The Art of Good Shooting

Major J. E. M. Ruffer

Royal Marines (Rtd)

Illustrated by

John Catchpole

David & Charles

NEWTON ABBOT LONDON

NORTH POMFRET (VT) VANCOUVER

ISBN 0 7153 7188 6

First published 1972
Extensively revised 1976

Photoset in 11 on 13 point Bembo
and printed in Great Britain by
Redwood Burn Limited
Trowbridge and Esher
for David & Charles (Publishers) Limited
Brunel House Newton Abbot Devon

Published in the United States of America
by David & Charles Inc
North Pomfret Vermont 05053 USA

Published in Canada
by Douglas David & Charles Limited
1875 Welch Street North Vancouver BC

The Art of Good Shooting

An expert shot – and one of the few really first-class shotgun coaches – Major Ruffer has written an essential guide to good practice with the shotgun. He covers country sport shooting and the no less exacting sport of clay pigeon shooting, showing how the same basic skills bring good results in each. While covering all the essentials of safety and etiquette when shooting, he explains that shooting is an art that can be taught and learned quickly. This book helps the beginner to become a good and safe shot, and helps experienced guns to eliminate hitherto unsuspected faults.

Widen Your Horizons with this new series

Remember that we cater for all interests. See for yourself with our expanding list of titles.

Places to see

Scottish Islands – Tom Weir
Dartmoor – Crispin Gill

Leisure activities

Railways for Pleasure – Geoffrey Body
Good Photography Made Easy – Derek Watkins
Looking at Churches – David Bowen

Sporting

Archery for All – Daniel Roberts

Holidays

Pony Trekking – Edward Hart

Forthcoming titles

Exmoor – Colin Jones
Sea Fishing for Fun – Alan Wrangles
A Guide to Safe Rock Climbing – Patrick Scrivenor
Rowing for Everyone – Christopher Chant

Contents

Introduction

Books on sport are usually written by tournament winners, or those most successful in competitions. They are, of course, the acknowledged experts. But it is one thing to be good at a sport, and quite another to be able to tell other people how to do it.

There are, on the other hand, people who are really keen on a sport, often quite good at it, and who also have the great asset so far as others are concerned that they enjoy teaching. I belong to this category.

And if you enjoy teaching, you cannot fail to become quite good at it. This is perhaps because the whole business of teaching makes you tackle the problem from a different angle. The average shot goes to a coach to find out what he is doing WRONG. I – if I can teach at all – have to analyse everything down so that it is done correctly. In short, I work for what is RIGHT.

We all know the days when we can hit anything that comes. Most of us do not worry about days like this; but this is just when I, as an instructor, get down to thinking and analysing what I have been doing to make things go right. And so I now know what has got to be done to shoot correctly. In short, I can make the good days repeat. And, after all, the definition of a good shot is the man who shoots well when he is shooting badly.

There is one step further for any instructor, and that is to convey his knowledge to his pupil. This is comparatively easy with young people, and sometimes almost impossible with older people. This is basically because the older person thinks he is doing something that he has been told – is positively certain of it – when, in fact, he is not doing it at all. In short, merely to read this book would be a waste of time. *You must practise what is preached.*

Practising can be done in your bedroom, by yourself with the help of a looking-glass, and you should certainly not despise the clay pigeon and the shooting school. I, myself, do as much shooting as I can, and frequently go to a shooting school. Occasionally when out shooting, I meet the really first-class shot (of whom there are remarkably few!) and when I later mention his name to my shooting instructor, that good shot is invariably well known at the shooting schools. If *he* thinks it worth it, how much more profitable would it be to us lesser mortals?

No one man is a better shot than another! It is simply that the good shot makes it easier for himself, and this is an art that can be taught, and learnt quite easily.

This may not be believed. Someone will quickly tell of exceptions. Take for example, they will say, the few men and boys who have very bad co-ordination. They cannot shoot well, and never will. This does not disprove what I have said: that to be a good shot you have only to make it easier for yourself. Some people find the rules which make it easier for themselves, hard to learn; they merely take longer to become good shots.

Young people, of course, can very soon become good shots. They learn quickly and, what is more, they never forget. I once coached a seventeen-year-old boy who had never shot before. I told him what to do, and he did it exactly. He never missed. He never looked as if he would miss. (He did not come back. He was not very keen on shooting – a pity!)

You may not believe that it is *only* making it easier for yourself, that makes you a good shot. Let me give you an example of what I mean. I was out one day at Grantham where there was one young man shooting, who played cricket for England. He did not hit much. The next-door gun, who was a port-sodden old boy of sixty, scarcely missed anything all day. That man, although pathetically unfit, having slow reactions, and being half blind, knew enough about making it easier for himself to be able to shoot well. The young man did not know, and in spite of his complete physical fitness, inevitably shot badly. Think how well he could have shot if he had known the tricks of the trade.

Some of us know the day when one cannot miss. Equally we all know the day when one is even anxious that the birds do not come our way. The average shot is somewhere in between, and knows both ecstasy and despair.

Remember the definition of a good shot is the man who shoots well when he is shooting badly. This book will teach you never to shoot badly, and you will then quickly get a reputation – for what that is worth – of being a good shot. It is interesting that people always notice that man who is shooting well, and often do not spot the man 'off his day'. Not 'interesting' perhaps, so much as merciful.

1 Handling Your Gun

Holding your gun

There is, as ever, a correct and an incorrect way of holding a gun, by which I mean holding the gun preparatory to mounting it to your cheek and shoulder. I do not mean how to carry it, a subject dealt with in a later chapter.

I am going to assume that you shoot from the right shoulder. (If you shoot from the left, then for left hand read right hand throughout.) The left hand holds the gun at the fore-end. The actual position on the fore-end, or beyond even on the barrels, is important and we will discuss this in a moment.

Try and keep the thumb and fingers off the top of the barrels. Although I will repeatedly say that you do *NOT* look at the gun barrels when you are pointing and mounting (and firing) at the birds, a 'heavy' grip with fingers and thumb on top of the barrels tends to distort one's instinctive pointing sense, so keep them out of the way.

The right hand grasps the small of the butt, with the forefinger – trigger finger – on the trigger guard. The right hand should tend to be under the gun; if it is not, it will force the right elbow up as the gun comes into the cheek and shoulder. This, in turn, will tend to make it difficult to push the gun forward towards the bird. You will tend to *lift* the gun, instead of *pushing* it towards the bird. So let us make it easy for ourselves, and keep the right hand under, rather than on top of, the gun.

The thumb must be round the stock, not on top. There is a tendency, as you move the safety-catch from 'safe' prior to firing, for the thumb to remain there. If this is done, there are three disadvantageous effects:

(a) You lose slight control with the right hand.

(b) Under certain conditions – slack grip, too short a stock – the recoil will cause the end of the top lever to be forced back on to the end of your right thumb, possibly bruising it badly or even splitting the thumb.

(c) If your thumb is left on the 'safety-catch', the recoil of the first shot

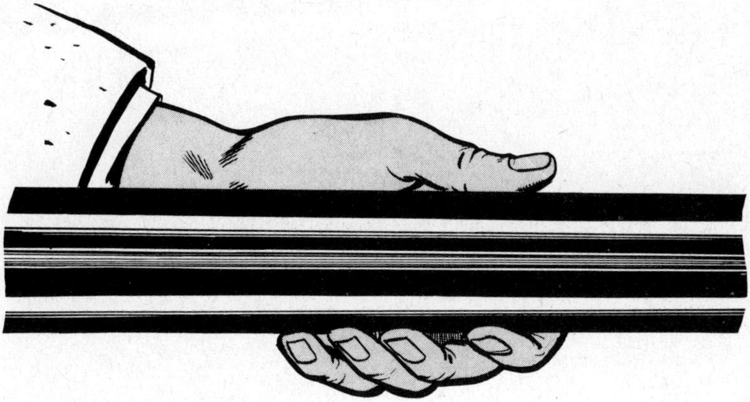

Try to keep the thumb off the top of the barrels

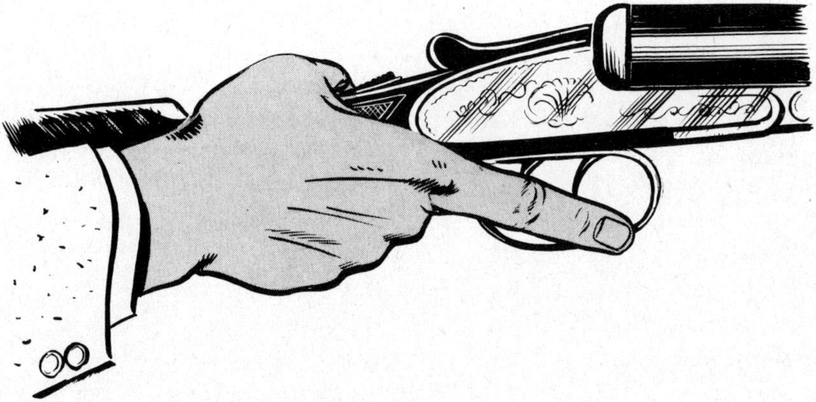

The right hand grasps the small of the butt, with the forefinger on the trigger guard. The hand should tend to be under the gun. The thumb must be round the stock, not on top

may well cause you unknowingly to re-apply the safety-catch, and then you are unable to fire the second barrel. As this happens without your being aware of it, you may think the gun is defective, and it can come quite expensive having a perfectly good safety-catch 'repaired'.

Do not have the right hand too far forward; that is, with the rear of the trigger-guard pressing hard up against the second finger. This is sometimes done so that the front trigger may be pulled with the *joint* of the first finger. Make sure that you pull the trigger with the ball of the first finger; to achieve this, you will have to pull your right hand back a shade. Then all bruising of the second finger from the back of the trigger guard will disappear.

Now where to place your left hand on the fore-end. Mount the gun by pointing and pushing the gun towards the target. The butt should just clear your clothing as it comes up into your shoulder and cheek. If it seems to catch, bring the left hand back a bit. If it obviously clears the clothing by a good gap, push your left hand a little further up the barrels.

Provided the length of the stock is about right, you can thus compensate for wearing heavy shooting clothes or not, simply by altering the position of your left hand on the barrels. More important, this is the best way of compensating for shooting with the same gun with longer arms, which occurs in the case of a growing boy.

The length of the stock should allow you to hold the gun towards the front of the fore-end. If the stock is much too long, you will be forced to hold the gun with the left hand too far back; and at once you can feel that the gun is more difficult to control.

It is also important to adopt a good position for the gun as soon as you realise that game is about to get up, or is approaching. Admittedly, it is virtually impossible to be sure when game is 'about to get up' – and this is one of the reasons why rough shooting or walking-up is more difficult than many would have us believe. All the same, if you do get warning – and you usually do, at least in the case of driven game – then it will pay you to adopt a position that will help you even before the bird is seen.

The object of good mounting is to get the gun pointing and moving towards the bird as soon as possible. You must therefore adopt a preliminary position to ensure that the barrels have as short a distance to go to the bird as possible – the shorter the better.

Take up a position with the gun roughly horizontal, with the stock tucked and gripped under the right fore-arm. In the case of a high bird approaching, adopt the same position with the barrels cocked up a bit. The barrels now have only a short distance to go to any bird approaching, and you can more easily fulfil the criterion of mounting with the bird. (See following section on Gun Mounting.)

Many of us start off with the barrels pointing downwards. Consider how far the barrels have to move before they are pointing at the bird, and how much more difficult it becomes to point and push forward at the bird. So make it easier for yourself by starting with the gun somewhere near where the bird is going to be.

Do not stand with the gun at the 'high port' position, especially when expecting a lowish bird. The barrels then have to come *down* towards the bird, whereas the bird, if it is up in the air at all, appears to require the barrels to be moving *up* to keep with it. This 'high port' position, therefore, does not make it easier for you, though it is often adopted by the pheasant shot when shooting grouse for the first time. When you see him with his gun like this on a grouse moor, it is a fairly safe bet that he is about to make a hash of his first day's grouse shooting.

Adopt the position I have suggested and you can then go straight to the bird with the minimum of effort. You are making it easy for yourself. There are, of course, many occasions when this position just is not possible, as when trying to keep hidden and often when walking-up. In these cases, you must accept the disadvantage but, whatever you do, do not accept it when you do not have to.

Gun mounting

A recent article in a shooting magazine claimed that good gun mounting was half the battle to good shooting. The author was wrong: it is very nearly all the battle. Learn good and correct gun mounting, and you are going a very long way down the road to the goal of making it easy for yourself.

The explanation of how to do it correctly is not easy and may sound slightly complicated, but once understood the execution of correct gun mounting will present no difficulties.

The snag of course is that the easiest way of shooting never has been

The 'ready' position. Gun roughly horizontal pointing to where you expect the bird; stock tucked and gripped under the fore-arm

taught (so far as I know). No one yet has really got down to the fundamentals of teaching people how to use the splendid co-ordination – apparently designed specifically for shooting! – which all of us possess.

One factor is paramount: *Your gun must be with the bird all the time you mount*. To achieve this, your gun mounting must be unhurried. The man who snatches his gun to his shoulder has as much chance of keeping the gun with the bird as he mounts as swimming the Channel with roller skates.

To achieve this 'gun with the bird' effect, you must point your gun deliberately at the bird as you mount. Just as you instinctively straighten your arm when you point with your finger, so you should feel as if you were straightening your arms towards the target as you mount. It should feel as if you were pushing your gun forward towards the bird – as indeed you are. And you must do this instinctively; you must *not* look at your barrels.

You may ask how anyone can point his gun at the target before it gets to his shoulder and without looking at the barrels. Well, point with your finger at any object in your room; instinctively you point straight at the object (straightening your arm as you do so), without looking at your finger. And if you subsequently sight along your finger, you will find you are dead on.

The same applies if you visualise the gun barrels as your finger. Point them at the bird, by pushing the gun forward, making a strong effort to point at the bird *all the time you are mounting*. This is the really difficult part; not that it is difficult to *do* but the trouble is that you *think* you are pointing at the bird all the time you are mounting, when you are not!

Imagine you are shooting with a gun that is capable of projecting a very fast jet of water from its barrel. Mount the gun keeping the imaginary jet of water playing on the bird.

To keep the jet of water on the bird would be easy enough.

And it is equally easy if the jet of water is imaginary!

You can practise this quite easily. It is possible to buy a form of torch which can be inserted in the bore of your gun, and which can then project a spot of light to show where the gun is pointing.

Select an object in your room – an ornament on the mantelpiece, a corner of the ceiling and walls for example – and with the gun in the 'ready' position (page 12), point it so that the light shines on the object.

Now mount the gun to your shoulder and cheek, so that the light does not leave the object at any point in the mounting. Try it slowly at first: but soon (within a couple of minutes), you will be able to mount the gun as quickly as you like without the light wavering from the object. When you can do this, you are more than well on the way to becoming a good shot.

Of course, the object is not moving; but it is almost as easy, even if it is.

Make sure your gun is unloaded and go and try in the garden; point the gun as you mount at any bird in flight and see how easy it is. Now get a friend to stand behind you and ask him if you were 'with' the bird as you mounted. He may say:

(a) Yes. (Unlikely the first two or three times!)
(b) That you mounted so quickly he could not see. (You snatched the gun up – do it slower!)
(c) You dipped the barrels below the bird, as you *raised* the butt into your shoulder. (You must *push* the gun towards the bird.)

I have tried not to use the word 'slowly' in talking about gun mounting as the impression I want to convey is 'unhurried'. The slower your mounting (*before* it gets into your shoulder), the easier it is to mount with the bird. You will not jerk the barrels off the bird, and you can concentrate on mounting smoothly and unhurriedly with the bird. But, you may say, the bird does not give you time for all this. (It nearly always does.) The point I am making – rather laboriously perhaps – is that you must learn to do it properly, and it is easier if you start slowly. So choose a bird in your garden that is some distance away and coming slowly towards you so that you have sufficient time to practise on it.

Notice that I have said mount the gun 'with the bird', and this is meant literally – certainly with no lead yet. Now, *as the gun comes into the shoulder*, it is (if you are still 'with' the bird) easy to move the gun fractionally ahead of the bird and pull the trigger. This is really easy, as the 'extra' movement is minute at the gun end – your end.

When you do this, you quite unconsciously carry out all the maxims that the gun experts say should be observed when shooting:

You have not checked. You cannot if you keep with the bird. You are keeping the gun moving. Vital!

Your gun must be with the bird all the time you mount

Point your gun deliberately at the bird as you mount

Your gun must be on the target all the time you mount

You are achieving an accelerating movement.

You are pulling the trigger when the gun comes into the shoulder, and not dwelling on aim with the gun in your shoulder.

All this sounds appallingly complicated in the limited time you have got when the bird is in shot, or approaching the shot. It is not. All you are doing, really, is to slow down your mounting and speed up your trigger pull, so gaining a very great advantage.

As an example of how this works, let us assume that a partridge is flying roughly towards you at 40mph, and you see him well out. If you put your gun with him when he is forty yards away and, mounting with the bird, shoot him when he is twenty yards out, you will have had the gun with him for one second. Your mounting has lasted one second.

If you had flung up the gun in the 'old fashioned' way and shot as soon as the 'picture' was correct, you would have been with him for only about one-tenth of a second. All things being equal, which method is likely to succeed more often?

By mounting 'with' the bird, you have a much longer time to get the picture right. You are, in effect, aiming while you are mounting, which makes the whole business much more precise and easy. Using this method, you seem to have plenty of time. And how often have we said that about the really good shots? This is how they do it, even if they do not realise it!

Once you have mastered the unhurried mounting of the gun with the bird, you can then consider speeding it up a bit, although this is not usually necessary. If you point the gun at the bird with your left hand, all you now have to do is to raise the butt from about the level of your chest to your cheek and shoulder. If we assume that the left hand is holding the gun at about the point of balance, then all the strong right forearm and hand has to do is to raise the butt (weighing about 3lb) about six inches into the cheek and shoulder. Obviously this can be done very quickly. But this is where you must be careful, for there is a strong tendency for the barrels to go down, off the target, as the butt comes into your shoulder. This can, and must, be counteracted by a push forward towards the target as the butt comes up. A glance at the sketches on pages 15–17 will show how the gun 'locks on' to the bird and stays as you mount. Imagine you have a bayonet on the end of the gun and try and push it into the bird as you are mounting, so that it will go right into the bird as the gun comes into shoulder and cheek. (See p 20.)

Once you have learnt to do it correctly, you can mount the gun slowly or quickly, as you wish, and I would suggest that you vary the speed of the mounting according to the time the bird gives you. Thus for a high pheasant coming from a long way off, a slower unhurried mounting will enable you to achieve the precision that such a bird requires. The driven grouse coming down wind requires a sharper, but still unhurried mounting with the bird.

If what I say about mounting the gun is correct, it will 'work' for all types of shot. It *must* do so to be correct. You cannot adopt a 'pheasant' style for pheasants, and a 'grouse' style for grouse, or even a 'rabbit' style for rabbits. What works for one, must work for all.

When the gun comes into the shoulder and cheek, pull the trigger for better or for worse! You will hit the bird. There is no need for last minute corrections – trust your eye and your mounting, and you will hit. If this is all you have to do, it all becomes easier.

If you mount the gun, and *then* aim with the gun already in your cheek and shoulder, you will never shoot well or quickly, or in good style. You are then using the gun like a rifle. This is 'poking', which, since it is only making things harder for you, is to be avoided at all costs.

Style is very difficult to define, but basically good style looks right, and bad style wrong. Aiming with the gun in your shoulder looks wrong; it is bad style. Using such a style makes it difficult for yourself, for as your brain says 'fire, you check – a fact of which you are quite unconscious. You are thus employing a slowing-down swing of your gun, instead of an accelerating swing.

The proper method of mounting with the bird makes it so easy that there is a strong feeling that it is just too easy merely to pull the trigger when the gun comes up. Surely there must be a period of adjustment to make sure that the aim or 'picture' is correct. All I can say is that no such adjustment is necessary if you mount the gun in the manner I have described. Pull the trigger and if you have mounted correctly you will kill the bird. If you funk the immediate trigger pull (must make sure!) you will check unconsciously. To try to make sure is fatal; you are losing all the advantage gained, besides making a miss almost inevitable.

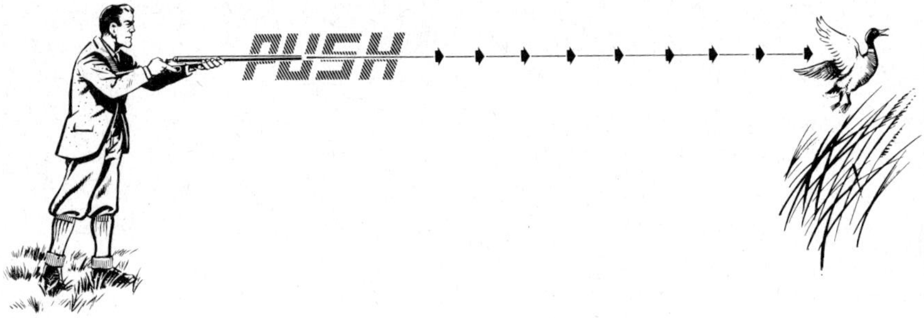

Imagine you have a bayonet on the end of the gun and try and push it into the bird as you are mounting

'Fire as soon as the gun comes into your cheek and shoulder.' So many of us are so used to mounting the gun quickly and then aiming that our first efforts to comply with this instruction, simply means a quick snatch and 'Bang', with the gun pointing anywhere. So let me repeat: you must mount with the bird – this is axiomatic. Watch the really class shot as a bird approaches. The barrels go straight to the bird and stay with it, the butt comes smoothly up, and the bird collapses. The gun has moved with absolute rock-like precision to the bird and stayed there. The barrels are 'on' and kept on with the push or slow prod of the left hand as the butt comes up. The man behind the gun is looking fixedly at the bird, and makes no attempt to correct his aim when the gun is mounted. He pulls the trigger. He knows from experience he will kill, though even he did not believe it at first!

To shoot well like this is easy, and all you have to do is to do it! The only trouble is that you may *think* you are doing everything correctly, whereas in fact you are not. Here, then, are some of the snags which may be deceiving you.

Look at the bird – not at your barrels. You may ask 'How can I point the barrels at the bird as I am mounting, if I don't look at the barrels?' I repeat that you do not look at your finger when you are pointing, nor do you look at a tennis racquet or cricket bat when you are hitting the ball. There is no need to! You look at the ball. . .

So look at the bird as you mount with it.

Push or point the gun at the bird, in the same way as you point with your finger. This is in contradiction to lifting the gun to the target. If you lift the gun to a low bird, the momentum of two arms and the gun moving upwards will tend to take the gun over a low-flying bird and you will have to correct, or you will miss over the top. In any case, you will be breaking the rule of keeping the gun pointing at the bird while you mount. Furthermore, lifting will almost inevitably cause the barrels to dip down as you mount the butt to your cheek. So do not lift the gun to the bird: point it by pushing it at the bird.

It was a well known shot who first said that the position adopted by the good shot before mounting his gun, was that of a boxer. How right he is!

Adopt it without a gun in your hands and see if it feels right. Then take up your gun, and hold the position again. If you are left-handed, then the 'southpaw' stance is for you.

Now to shoot well, all you do is to punch the target with the old fashioned Straight Left. Your body goes forward slightly with the blow, your right hand is guarding your chin; your head has not moved.

You need not (in fact must not) do it very quickly as you would when boxing, but deliberately. I frequently find myself saying when coaching 'Punch it in the nose'. After the shot, I say 'Now do it like that, only more deliberately'.

With this 'boxing' advice, you will be doing what I advocate – push and point at the target. Everything falls into position – the movement of the gun, the correct position of the body and head, and (of course!) correct footwork.

Mount the gun by pointing it at the bird unhurriedly. If you snatch the gun to the shoulder (as most of us do), you cannot keep the gun on the bird as you mount, and you will have to aim after you get the gun up – fatal!

Pull the trigger as the gun comes into your shoulder and cheek. If you have mounted with the bird, you have done your aiming; you have finished all the difficult part. All you then have to do is to pull the trigger. If, on the other hand, you lose your nerve and try to make sure, you are aiming with the gun in your shoulder – again fatal!

To sum up:

(a) THE ACTUAL MOUNTING OF THE GUN WITH THE BIRD IS VITAL. THIS IS WHEN YOU ARE AIMING. TO GET THE MAXIMUM VALUE, DO NOT HURRY THIS.

YOU SELDOM HAVE TO, WHATEVER YOU MAY FEEL.

(b) PULL THE TRIGGER AS THE GUN GETS TO YOUR SHOULDER AND CHEEK.

You may take a bit longer over (a) – time well spent, but you will save time over (b) – time well saved.

Gun fit

Most good English gunmakers insist that a perfectly fitting gun is essential to good shooting. Americans, on the other hand, are often very good shots yet almost never have their guns fitted to them.

Both cannot be right – and yet can they?

You will have heard of the very keen shot who lost the sight of his right eye. He immediately had a gun made with cross-eyed stock so that he could shoot from his right shoulder using his left eye. To any normal person picking up the gun, it appeared to point anywhere but where he was looking. The instructor came along and, in front of an audience fired a few shots at some 'high pheasant' clays. He hit every one. Naturally he was asked 'How on earth . . .?' His simple reply: 'Closed my right eye'.

The object of a well-fitting gun is to ensure that when it is mounted correctly to your shoulder it will then be pointing where you are looking and thus will shoot to this point. What do we mean by 'mounted correctly'? I would describe this as the gun bedded well into the cheek, assuming that the head has not moved whilst the gun is being mounted, and with the butt in the shoulder and not on the arm. And for 'fitting' to mean anything, the gun must be mounted exactly like this *every* time. The vast majority of us, of course, do no such thing, although we often think we do.

The gun often does not come up to the shoulder, it often does not come into the cheek. If it does come into the cheek, we have probably moved our head to get it there. And so on . . . ad infinitum.

To 'fit' a gun to such a man is patently a waste of time. Of course, we can be sure that it is roughly right – the approximate length of stock and so on, but before a gun can be 'fitted' and all the attendant benefits enjoyed, we must learn the correct position of the gun in the shoulder. And this must be achieved every time – the slow deliberate shot, the snap shot, the curling grouse shot, the hare going away – every time the gun must come up to the correct position, the same position.

English gun with cast-off allows head to be kept still

American 'mass-produced' gun with no cast-off, requires head to be tilted

How then can this be correct for Americans, or those who do not have their guns fitted? The answer is that the American has learnt to bring his gun up into the same position every time, and then has learnt to correct for any misfit by moving his head to make the necessary adjustment, or shooting slightly high, or whatever. But this makes it slightly harder for him, and breaks our rule that we must make things easier for ourselves.

So, learn to mount correctly every time, and a correctly fitted gun will then make it easier for you.

For a youngster, of course, gun fit can only confer a temporary benefit since, as a young boy grows, he is getting broader, and his arms longer. This latter point is most important. Every holiday I see lots of young boys shooting with the same guns as they had the holiday before. I know without looking that they will miss high, because their stock will be too short. And they always do! As the young man mounts the gun, you will see a gap between the butt and his shoulder. He then has to pull it back to get it into his shoulder. The cure is either for him to hold the gun with his left hand (assuming that he is shooting from his right shoulder) further towards the end of the barrels, or to fit a rubber pad on the end of the stock. This is not always very satisfactory as the pad is sometimes inclined to wobble; also the rubber is apt to catch in clothing and prevent the butt from coming right up. Since our philosophy is to make things as easy for ourselves as possible, think hard before you fit a rubber pad.

You will now have realised that the position of the gun in your shoulder:

(a) Must be the same every time you mount. If it is not, you are introducing a variable; since you are usually unconscious of this, it is one reason for the 'unaccountable' miss.

(b) When the gun is in your shoulder correctly, it should be pointing where you are looking without you having to correct it.

Now, how to find out whether these two factors are correct for you? The answer, as usual, is to try and see.

Mount the gun quickly (without aiming) at a prominent object, or branch, or top of a hedge; then, keeping everything still except your arms, lower the gun to the 'trail' position. Are you now in a natural standing position, or is your head pushed forward and down? Put another way, do you normally walk about with your head in the

When the gun is in your shoulder correctly, it should be pointing where you are looking

If you find a bruise on the top of your arm, the butt was not in your shoulder but out to the right on your arm

Mount the gun quickly . . . and see if you are in a natural standing position

. . . or is your head pushed forward and down?

position it was left in when you lowered your gun? If not, you are moving your head and making the gun come into the wrong position in your shoulder. You are not making things easier for yourself.

After shooting several shots, do you find a bruise the next morning on the top of your arm? I frequently do, and it means that the butt was not into your shoulder, but out to the right on your arm. If the butt was too far right, the barrels will be too far left, and you will tend to miss there.

Next time you pull your trigger, ask yourself 'Is my gun really into my cheek?' Remember, it is possible to feel the bump of recoil on your cheek, but the gun was not there when it went off. What you have got to say to yourself is: 'The stock is into my cheek – BANG – and I have kept it there'. For it is quite possible to put the stock into your cheek, then at the last moment unconsciously to lift your cheek off the stock (to see where you have missed?). And if you were asked subsequently whether the gun was into your cheek when you fired, you would be prepared to bet your life that it was. Do not: you would lose!

Finally, mount the gun at any prominent stationary object – chimney pot, branch, or anything you like. Mount it quickly without aiming, *keeping both eyes open*. Then, without moving the gun, squint along the barrels as if it were a rifle and see where it is pointing. If 'on', you are all right. If you are out to the left of the target, read the section on 'Master Eye' in Chapter 2. If you are consistently high/low or otherwise off the target, the fit of your gun probably wants looking at.

If you want gun-fitting to benefit you, you must practise.

Pick up your gun and mount it into the correct position in your shoulder and cheek five times every day. You can do this indoors.

Do it slowly, to make sure that your head is not moving. Do it quickly in front of a mirror to see how much your head *has* moved. Do it again quickly without moving your head.

Do it on Monday, Tuesday, Wednesday . . . and so on, every day. When you forget, read the chapter on Practising.

One might sum up this section by saying that the 'fit' of a gun is desirable, but not vital. If you mount the gun correctly (and therefore in the same place) every time, a correctly-fitted gun will make shooting easier for you, and is then of great benefit. But correct mounting every time is more important than gun fit.

Footwork

Footwork – good footwork – is not vital to successful shooting. Think of the wildfowler stuck in the mud; he has not got any footwork. Or the rough shooter in roots – not much footwork there.

But we are back to our old cry: 'Let us do everything we possibly can to make shooting easier. Where you cannot move your feet effectively, then you will obviously have to do without the real help that good footwork can give. But do not let us do without it unless we must.

You should stand with your feet quite close together, your heels, say, about 9–12in apart, and they should be pointing at an angle of about 45 degrees, to your right. The reason for this is to enable you to pivot easily with the weight on one foot. If your feet are a long way apart, you will find it difficult to pivot, because both feet then tend to remain flat-footed on the ground. Pivoting to right or left, then, depends solely on the flexibility of the hips; and not all of us have any hips visibly and flexibly left. We are thus not making it easy for ourselves, if the feet are too far apart.

I have two shooting books, one of which says categorically that, for a high pheasant, the weight should be on the left foot, while the other book says on the right foot. Both cannot be right – surely? But I think they can! We can translate both 'rules' as weight on *one* foot, not on both. This makes sense to me, and I think it will to you. With the feet close together, it is easy to transfer the weight onto one foot, and this is what you must do.

The other premise I put forward was that the feet should be pointing an at angle of about 45 degrees to your right. There are obviously two extremes from this – one with the feet 'sideways'; that is in the Army stand-at-ease position; and the other with the feet one in front of the other. There are pretty heavy disadvantages with both extremes, which we can avoid with our 45 degrees compromise.

Let us see. Stand with your feet 'sideways' to your front – as if 'standing at ease'. Now raise both arms in front of you (if you are holding a gun – so much the better). You *must* lean back to counteract the weight of your arms and gun, or you will fall flat on your face. But to lean back and shoot from off your heels makes shooting very difficult. You cannot turn or pivot, and if you are pushing the gun towards the bird all the time, as I advocate, your body must follow as you push the

Your feet should be quite close together to enable you to pivot easily with the weight on one foot

gun forward. And so it should. With a low bird, this means leaning forward; which is impossible without falling over if your feet are 'sideways'. With a high bird, pushing the gun at the bird as you mount means reaching up, and even this is difficult with the sideways stance if the bird is in front of you at all. So *not* sideways.

The other extreme is one foot behind the other, and more people get into this position than they realise. (Do you? Of course not! . . . but have a look, all the same.) If you do do this, it will tend to push your left shoulder towards a bird coming from your front – and more important, your right shoulder away from such a bird. Now as you mount at the bird in front, your cheek will tend to push the butt outwards, so that with the right shoulder back, the butt mounts on the top of your right arm, and not in your shoulder. You will miss – and 'unaccountably', too!

Now the weight on one foot. If you stand with the weight on your left foot, your left leg and body can become an upright shaft about which your body can rotate easily. 'Easily' is still the operative word – make it easy for yourself. You can then swing right or left, upwards or downwards, always able to push the gun at the bird as you mount. Your weight will be on *one* foot, and so you can turn easily.

If you prefer to move your weight on to the right foot for a bird on your right, and so on, there is no objection. The weight must basically be mostly on *one* foot when you are shooting. This means that you are always leaning towards the bird when you are shooting. That is, leaning down and forward at rabbits, forward at, say, low-flying grouse, and reaching up and towards the high bird. All this follows from the instruction to push the gun at the bird when mounting. And this is correct.

You must not overdo it, of course; there is obviously a limit as to how far forward you can lean at a low bird. However, the principle stands.

There are also psychological factors working against you. As you mount your gun in front of you, one's instinct is to lean back to counteract the weight. Good footwork will compensate for this.

Similarly, when a fast, low bird comes at you, it is quite difficult psychologically to push the gun and yourself towards it. Yet you must, and your footwork must allow you to do so. It is, after all, difficult enough to overcome the instincts which will tend to make you mount your gun wrongly. Do not make it well nigh impossible with bad footwork.

2 Firing Your Gun

Lead or forward allowance

It is an incontrovertible fact that lead, or forward allowance, is required in order to hit a moving bird. The amount of lead depends on several factors, but mainly on the speed of the bird and the angle to you at which it is flying.

In short, the gun has to be ahead of the target to a greater or lesser degree when the trigger is pulled – or to be more pedantically accurate, when the shot leaves the barrel. What the necessary lead looks like to you may well vary from what it looks like to me, or to someone else. If we are both (for argument's sake), firing at the same bird from the same position and kill it, the actual lead given by both of us will be the same, obviously. But you may say you gave it six feet; I may think I only gave it a few inches. What the correct lead is, is utterly immaterial here; what I am concerned about is what the correct lead looks like to *you*.

That the correct lead does look different to different people is I am sure, true, and I would even say that the correct lead so far as one person is concerned may well seem to vary from day to day. Have you ever noticed how, at the end of one day, you were hitting them with comparatively little lead, whereas at the beginning of the next day out, you are clearly behind with what looks like the same lead, and have to give more?

The answer is not a corroded liver, or a thick (or perhaps thin) night the night before. It is in how you mount your gun. If you mount your gun correctly, the apparent lead you have to give for a particular bird will not vary for you from day to day, or hour to hour, or ever.

In a previous chapter you were urged always to achieve an accelerating swing by mounting the gun with the bird, and then almost instinctively going slightly ahead as – and NOT after – the gun comes into cheek and shoulder. With an accelerating swing, the apparent lead always appears a good deal less than when you achieve a swing that is (unknown to you) slowing down.

In fact, when mounting correctly for fast birds fairly close to, you appear to need no lead at all. This is because when the bird is close to, you are moving your gun quickly if you are with the bird as you mount, and so unconsciously give the correct lead as you *apparently* shoot straight at it.

Indeed, when you start mounting correctly but still give the lead you used to when you were mounting the gun any old how, you will tend to miss in front.

Close and fast birds, then, can be shot by apparently pointing straight at them, but some lead (to you) is required for the high bird, and the bird well out. Remember, you must mount with the bird – *not* ahead – and as (and only as) the gun comes into cheek and shoulder the gun can be moved fractionally ahead and the trigger pulled.

Take care not to mount ahead of the bird, because then there will be no acceleration to the swing. Mount with and at the bird. Take care to see that any lead is smoothly 'added' as the gun comes into your cheek and shoulder. Take care not to give too much lead; if you are mounting well, as you have been taught, the lead becomes a minor factor; it *feels* like a few inches as the gun is kept going.

The whole thing is being made easier for you.

Poking

'Poking' is a word that is used frequently in shooting, and it has probably save the lives of more game and of anything else that is shot at than any other fault in shooting.

We all know that poking in the shooting sense is wrong; in fact, it is considered 'bad form' to be guilty of it. It is the dirty word of shooting. Everybody, almost instinctively, does what they can to avoid being accused of this sin, and yet nearly everybody commits it to a greater or lesser degree.

Let us see what poking really is. It is aiming with the gun already mounted into the cheek and shoulder. In a bad case, a gun will mount his weapon quickly, and then spend quite a long time dwelling on the bird in order to make sure that he will hit it. This is poking.

Now, if you come to think of it, anybody who aims his gun after mounting it any old how, has to do just this – either quickly or slowly –

Correct gun mounting, side view; the butt mounts smoothly to the shoulder with the muzzles glued to the target

in order to correct his aim. In other words, if he snatches his gun to his shoulder and then has to correct his aim with the gun there in order to hit the bird, he is guilty of poking. If he does it slowly, he is poking for all to see; if he does it quickly, he is still, in fact, poking; but it is not quite so apparent!

So great is his fear of being accused of poking that a gun will often try to do everything as quickly as possible in order to escape any such accusation. How often have we heard somebody say that he can hit birds that come quickly at him, whereas the birds coming from a long way off present, to him, an insuperable problem? I have even heard of some guns who, seeing a high pheasant coming, will actually look at the ground until they judge the birds to be roughly overhead, and will then snap at it as it comes overhead.

Basically, all this is to avoid the accusation of poking. If they had never heard of the word, they would mount the gun any old how, and then correct the aim, slowly or quickly according to the speed of the bird. Although they would, in fact, still be guilty of poking – as they are now – they would be slightly more accurate shots than the man who, determined to avoid the accusation, snatches up his gun and fires in a hurry.

Another phrase that must be read in conjunction with poking is 'Take your Birds Early'. This phrase, too, has caused almost as many misses as the fear of poking. In effect, the average gun trying to obey this commandment does exactly the same as when he is trying to avoid poking. He snatches the gun to his shoulder, and (having made that mistake), shoots quickly.

But if you mount with the bird, and shoot when the gun gets to your cheek and shoulder, you will easily be able to take your bird early. The same drill as described in the section on Gun Mounting, but take the bird a little sooner. It will work!

You will see at once, too, that the instruction to 'fire as the gun comes into your shoulder' automatically prevents poking, or indeed ever being accused of it, however deliberately you are shooting. But we must remember that it is absolutely no good firing as the gun comes into the cheek and shoulder unless you have mounted with the bird.

All of us who mount in a hurry, any old how, are therefore nearly always guilty of poking because we have to correct our inaccurate aim *after* the gun has got to the shoulder. And the more we try to correct this by shooting quickly, the more inaccurate our shooting becomes. If we mount the gun with a quick snatch or, indeed, even if we mount the gun slowly without mounting it with the bird as we do so, then we are in trouble.

If you accused most experienced guns of poking, they would deny it with an oath. And yet this is exactly what they are doing! So be humble! Say to yourself 'Am I poking to a greater or lesser degree?' If you are not mounting the gun with the bird and shooting as the gun comes to your shoulder, you are, indeed, poking – with all the attendant evils thereof.

Thus, the only way to escape the accusation of poking is to mount the gun with the bird and fire the gun as it comes into your shoulder – and this method is precisely the course of action advocated throughout this book.

Special shots

A sound system or method of shooting must work for all types of shot, and in order to demonstrate that the method advocated in this book will always work I have proposed to deal with a few of the different types of target to which it can equally successfully be applied.

The Snap Shot: Let us suppose that you are shooting driven grouse and a bird suddenly appears towards your right, when you are looking towards your left. 'You have only time to lift up your gun and fire', you will say. This, of course, is just not true: if you have time 'to lift up your gun', you will have time (as an alternative) to push the gun instinctively *at* the bird and fire. And in this latter case you will do it quickly, (but unhurriedly), but this does not alter the fundamental correctness of it.

Point *at* the bird, and pull. In this case, that is all there is to it. But if you *lift* the gun up, it will be a fluke if you are 'with' it; it will be a fluke if you hit it.

Commonsense suggests that if you are short of time, you must do something 'quickly'. True, of course, but you must also be unhurried, for strange as it may seem, this will make you both more accurate and faster. Let me illustrate this with a true story.

An officer in one naval ship in which I was serving was in charge of a

Point at it . . .

. . . mount with it

. . . and this will happen

batch of young officers and very keen that they should beat the sailors at a skill in which the sailor was an untouchable expert. At this time, there was a murderous contraption known as a '6-inch loader', which simulated the loading and firing of a 6in gun, with its 100lb projectiles. The Navy, being what it was, used to run 6in loader competitions, which were competed for with great determination by all ships – and which, incidentally, greatly improved the gunnery of the fleet.

The young officers gradually improved their skill with early morning practice, and got their time for ten rounds down to 52 seconds, which was very good, since the Navy record was approximately 50 seconds. To achieve a 52-second time, the young officers were, of course, flat out, lifting and ramming the heavy shells through the contraption in a mad rush. The 'drill' had become pretty instinctive by then.

The officer then said (Inspiration, did he but know it!), 'Let's try an unhurried run.' The time was 48 seconds! They eventually got down to 46.5 seconds, and this time has never been beaten (and never will be).

When you are out shooting, you have more time than you think. So be unhurried – always.

The Going Away Shot: How often do we hurry this shot. The bird is flying away, and soon will be out of shot. The gun is flung up – BANG! BANG! – the bird flies on, still leaving time for another shot, and probably two.

Put the gun smoothly *to* the bird, look at the bird, and 'pull' as the gun gets into the cheek and shoulder.

There is inevitably, at a bird going straight away from you, a tendency to aim the gun as if it were a rifle. You can only do this by adjusting the gun after it has got into the cheek and shoulder, and this we know is wrong. It is not possible to aim (in the accepted sense) if you fire as the gun comes into your cheek and shoulder, and since I insist on your firing immediately the gun is mounted, the inevitable tendency to snatch the gun to your shoulder (you have not time, you think) will cause you to miss.

Let me repeat: smoothly with the bird, look at the bird, and pull as the gun comes up to cheek and shoulder. It may seem slow at first to you, but it is not. And soon everyone will be saying that you always seem to have plenty of time.

The High Pheasant Shot: The high pheasant coming towards you gives you time – more than you may think. Use it! Mount your gun by pushing it up and at him, keep with him as you mount, and *as the gun comes into your cheek and shoulder,* (not before) come a little in front of him and pull.

He may be on a curve and be going fast; all this will be taken care of if you mount your gun with him. This is when you are picking up his course and speed; this is when you are 'aiming'.

Remember a really high bird is a difficult bird for anyone to hit. Make sure your technique is perfect; gun correctly mounted in your cheek and shoulder. If you are only slightly wrong, you will miss.

Try practising this by mounting your empty gun in the garden at a bird overhead; as it comes into your cheek and shoulder – stop! Then, keeping the gun where it is, come down with the gun still mounted in your cheek and shoulder, until the gun is horizontal. Are you in the correct position for a low shot? Head not moved? Gun into the shoulder and cheek perfectly? If not, you are going to miss your high birds. If all is well, you will kill them consistently.

Finally, do not be scared – or at least try not to be – by the anticipation of the bird coming straight for you, getting higher and higher! Use the time he gives you. Do not leave it until the last moment before mounting and try and make it into a snap shot; you are only making it harder for yourself if you do.

The Long Crossing Shot: Have you noticed how the moon, when new risen and close to the horizon, looks much larger than when it is high in the sky? It is, of course, the same size, but it *looks* bigger. In the same way, a bird near the ground looks bigger than when it is high up. This has two effects. A high bird looks higher than it is, and a low bird closer than it is. You will thus tend to miss the long, low crossing shot behind, because the long shot does require some forward allowance in your mind's eye.

There is a very strong tendency at these crossers to throw the gun up well ahead of the bird and pull the trigger. In this case, you may take it for granted – I have seen it so often – that the gun is quite stationary on firing. In other words, you are trying to intercept. The forward allowance then necessary is the distance the bird flies whilst the shot is getting there, *plus* the distance the bird flies during the time elapsing between your brain saying 'Fire!' and the shot getting out of the barrel.

Wrong. Bringing the butt to the shoulder makes the muzzles dip off the target, and forces you to over-correct. You have to aim with the gun mounted.
Note: unless you are a superb shot, you are very likely to be making this mistake.

This latter time is longer than the first, and will also vary from day to day, even shot to shot.

In such a case, to hit is practically impossible. You are not getting an accelerating movement, or even a slowing down one. You are getting none at all! So, mount with the bird, push the gun *at* him, and then as it comes into cheek and shoulder, go in front of him and keep the swing going. A little further than usual – the moon is 'bigger' low down.

Master eye

One eye is usually stronger than the other, and by that I do not necessarily mean better. I have always believed that, quite unconsciously, one uses one eye more than the other in much the same way as one is left- or right-handed, or left- or right-footed. This becomes particularly noticeable in shot-gun shooting, where the gun is fired from one side of the body and where both eyes are normally kept open. And sometimes a difficulty can arise.

Assuming that you shoot from the right shoulder, when you push and point the gun at the target, it will point at that target if your right eye is the master eye. If the left eye is the master eye, the gun will point to the left of the target, and by quite a large amount. The explanation of this is best given by the sketch on page 45.

As you will be unconscious of a left master eye – except by shooting badly – it is, perhaps, wise to check which is your master eye and here are two ways of doing this. One is to stand with your gun at the 'ready' position in front of a mirror, and then keeping both eyes open, mount your gun (without aiming your gun like a rifle) at your right eye – that is, the eye over the stock in the mirror. Now, without moving the gun, squint along the barrels, and see if it *is* pointing at your right eye. If it is, all is well. If it is pointing out to the left, as you see it, it may be that your left eye is the master eye.

The other and perhaps better way is to try with a friend. Open your unloaded gun, ask your friend to walk away about ten yards, face you and put his finger up in front of his right eye. Now, show him the empty chambers of your gun, close it and come to the 'ready' position. Mount your gun, without aiming, at his finger. If all is well, your friend will see the barrels pointing straight at his finger and eye. If he sees your barrels

When you push and point the gun at the target, your gun will point at that target if your right eye is the master eye

If the left eye is the master eye, the gun will point to the left of the target and by quite a large margin

Correct gun mounting, frontal view. See how the mounting barrels remain rock steady

Wrong. In the head-on view the dip of the barrels caused by over-hasty mounting is even more apparent

pointing out to his right (with the end of the barrels aligned with your left eye), then you are left-eye master, and something must be done about it.

It is quite possible, as you mount the gun, for your friend to see the barrels start to go to his right and then come round to his finger and eye, as you unconsciously correct. This may mean that you are *inclined* to be left-eyed. This, in turn, may mean that your left eye will take over in the case of birds to your left (and only then), or when you get tired.

We now appear to be in a hopelessly incurable state; but, fortunately, this is not so. The simplest cure is merely to close the left eye!

You must close it – or wink it just sufficiently to allow the other eye to take over – early on, as soon as you see the bird. If you leave it too late, you will start mounting with the left eye in control and, as a result, with the gun to the left of your target; then, as you close your left eye, you will realise this and have to correct. Close the left eye early and you will be able to mount correctly with the bird.

If you are truly left-eye master, and you do not like the idea of closing your left eye, you can instead:

(a) Shoot from your left shoulder, with a gun with cast-ON instead of cast-OFF.

(b) Have a cross-eyed stock built. These are both ugly and expensive.

Closing your left eye is certainly the simplest and cheapest solution, but it has a snag. First, you lose the slight advantage of having two eyes – so far as shooting is concerned, not very bothersome. Second, you forget! You will have to practise closing your left eye and, to start with, you will find it calls for quite a mental effort. I was once coaching someone, and told him to close his left eye; but he continued to miss left. I asked him if he was closing his eye and he said he was. So I slipped round to his left, and looked as he fired. He was doing no such thing – his left eye was wide open all the time. I might add that I then made certain that he did close his left eye, whereupon his shooting got slightly worse. I then found he was closing *both* eyes.

But closing or winking the left eye early on, is the complete cure. Inevitably, you will occasionally forget to do it, and especially at first. Remember this, and it will help – and it will help a great deal more if you practise closing your left eye when you practise mounting.

3 How to Practise

Practising

When people are frightened or excited, they almost invariably tend to act instinctively. You will be excited to some degree when you are shooting, and thus to some extent – perhaps more than you think – you will react instinctively.

Ask someone (if you dare) after a real 'hot' corner, if he was, for example, mounting his gun correctly every time; making sure of it. He will reply 'Yes', if he is a liar; or if he tells the truth, he will say 'No. I did not think of it; I had not time.' He had not time. Nor will you have time, and so you will do it wrong unless you have practised until it becomes instinctive. And this applies to all of us.

The really good shots go often to a shooting school – not, in their case, to learn how to shoot, but to practise. This may be an ideal way to do it, but it is not possible as a regular habit for everyone and, fortunately, we are all able to practise the various shooting movements quite easily at home, or even whilst in the office or waiting for a bus.

More than once I have been brought back to earth with a bump, following a hissed whisper of 'Driven Grouse' from my wife in church during a hymn, to realise that I had been practising my footwork, 'weight well forward on the left foot, pivoting easily'. I must have been taking them well out in front, beyond the Vicar, for it to have been noticed!

Some movements cannot be practised indoors. Mounting the gun in the way I suggest is one such movement, but it can be done in the garden, mounting 'dry' at small birds.

There are, after all, very few movements in shooting. They are basically:

Correct footwork.
Correct mounting of the gun.
Correct position of gun in the shoulder.
Correct moment of pulling the trigger.

Get these right by practice; so that you make the movements instinctively, without thinking, when you are shooting. Then and only then will you do them correctly, for you will find there is not time to think about them when you are actually out shooting. You will be excited – at least I hope so – and will react instinctively. And instinctively correct reactions can only be achieved by practice.

If you are a beginner, practice will show quick results, as you will find it easy to groove your mind into the correct course. If you are older and have shot for a bit, you will instinctively react in the bad old way if you do not persistently practise the new correct style. And what is worse, you may even think that you are doing it correctly while doing it wrong in the excitement of the moment.

It may seem scarcely credible that when you think you are actually carrying out a movement correctly, you are in fact doing no such thing. The truth is that in the excitement of the moment, you forget.

Let me prove this point. When I am coaching a pupil who (let us assume) is not putting the gun properly into his cheek, I will say to him 'Gun into the cheek', call for the bird, and he will shoot it. I can do this three or four times, each time reminding him about the gun coming into his cheek and he will do it correctly. When I think he has got it, I will call for a bird, without reminding him about his cheek and the gun. In nearly every case, he will mount as he used to, incorrectly with the gun not into his cheek, miss it, and then turn round and ask 'What on earth did I do wrong?' He forgot, because he was not reminded. The answer is practice.

The best practice of all is, of course, shooting at live game, the next best is clay pigeon practice, and the last is the 'dry' practice which I have advocated in this section, and which can be very effective.

Without practice, you will never become a good shot – however many books you read. With practice and intelligent guidance, you will become a good shot. It is as simple as that.

Clay pigeon shooting

There are various ways of practising by shooting at clay pigeons, and the most obvious is to join a clay pigeon club.

Some time ago, I thought I would go one better and start a clay pigeon club. It has prospered for six years, and we now have one member who shoots for England, and where we have entered a team for WAGBI or Game Fair shoots, we have either won or come second. Yet most of the team had virtually never fired a shot until they joined the club.

Because the club has improved our shooting out of all knowledge, and was so easy to form, it may be of interest to record how we set about forming it. But first let me make two points. One is that there was no other clay pigeon club nearby; and the other is that we decided from the outset that our object was to improve our game, or sporting shooting. We have not gone in for Down the Line shooting, and this concentration upon sporting shooting has necessarily influenced our set-up and equipment.

Three or four of us having decided to go ahead, we looked round for a suitable site and found it under two feet of snow in the winter of 1962/63. It consisted of a large field, the only building being a farm house about 250 yards away in one corner; and it had a disused quarry in the middle. It was this latter feature that decided us, as it made possible high driven 'birds'.

A meeting was called to elect a chairman, secretary, treasurer and committee, and with the help of the Clay Pigeon Shooting Association we drew up our rules, which will be found in appendix III to this book. They are self-explanatory, except for 'Temporary Membership' Rule 25, which was inserted so that schoolboys could join during their holidays.

Finance: We charge an entrance fee of two guineas ($5) and the annual subscription is the same. We vary these fees in the light of commonsense if a member is elected near the end of the financial year. Since we can buy cartridges and clays in bulk, we can offer members quite a large saving, even though we sell them cartridges at about 5p (12c) per hundred above what they cost us. Clays we charge at 2p (4c) each, although they cost us a fraction more than that. It is the 'pick up' of the missed clays at the end of the day that makes this profitable, too.

Lay-Out: Although we now have quite an elaborate layout, it came about gradually, and it would be as well to start with a simple set up which you can later expand to your own ideas, and with your own enthusiasm.

High Tower: Two of our members built a high tower of four telegraph poles, cross braced with two platforms. This they did in one day, and it cost us nothing. We enclosed a portion at the bottom of the tower, and this makes an ideal storeroom.

We have two international traps mounted at the top of the tower, and these throw the clays over the quarry. The quarry is about 40ft deep, and the tower traps about 30ft high, so the clays are about 25yds vertically overhead. At first sight, they *look* impossible to hit, but can be consistently 'killed' with a .410.

Grouse Butt: We dug an ordinary butt outside one side of the quarry, and 'fired' the clays from a mobile trap on the other side. This is virtually a level shot coming towards, but of course at different angles and heights. Some protection was arranged for the trapper.

Partridge Drive: The same members who built the high tower also arranged for bases on to which various traps could be quickly bolted. These bases consist of large oil drums, filled with cement, sunk slightly into the ground, and with bolts grouted into the top. Mounting a trap is then merely a matter of putting the trap onto the bolts, putting on the nuts and tightening up. We have put these bases at odd places as we thought necessary; all except one (in a useless position) are used regularly.

Probably the most popular position is at the head of the quarry, and out of sight of anyone standing in the quarry. The clays come over quickly at a height of about 30–40ft, and the angle can be varied also quite considerably.

Going-away Shot: This can be arranged from any of the mountings. If a longer shot is required, we have a shield which will protect the trapper when the gun wishes to go well back behind the trap.

Springing Teal: Another member built a steel attachment which bolts onto one of the concrete bases, and onto which the trap is, in its turn, bolted. This cocks the trap up at an angle of about 60/70 degrees. The trapper is protected by the 'going away' shield.

Mobile Trap: We purchased a pedal trap by Bowman, and this has been invaluable, although it is a bit heavy to move around. (Two men can carry it easily). It requires little effort to 'fire' it; (this is done by foot), and it is very quick. It is possible to get up to seven clays in the air at once; the velocity, angle and height of the clay can be quickly and easily adjusted. The trapper sits! We had a bit of trouble with one of the ratchets, but the answer is never to fire the trap without a clay in it. The service offered by Bowman is quite first class and cheap.

'Walkie-Talkies': I have long felt that shouting or whistling for clays to be thrown is out of date. If you are going to go in for driven-game practice, the trap is inevitably some way from the gun and often out of sight. Instead, we bought two 'walkie-talkies', and obtained the necessary licences. Apart from whip aerials getting broken and batteries running out, they are still working well after six years. They only weigh a pound or two each.

They are, of course, an enormous help. The trapper can be told what to do, and can communicate with the gun when required. It is not even necessary to speak when the coach or gun wants the clay to be thrown; if the 'transmit' button is pressed, this makes a 'plop and a hiss' in the trapper's receiver, which is signal enough for him to let a clay go. 'Walkie-talkies' are not of course, necessary for Down the Line, Going Away and Springing Teal shots, since the gun is so close to the trapper that a verbal call is easy and effective.

Coaching: The object of our clay pigeon club is to improve the shooting of the members. Unless you have someone in the club who is a first-class coach, members will improve their shooting but slowly, and will often reach a 'ceiling' well below the standard of marksmanship of which they may well be capable. As few of our members could afford the time to visit a first-class coach, we decided to invite one to come to us, and Rex Gage, of Holland & Holland, has now been to coach our members many times. We arranged that he should coach them in pairs for an hour, at a weekend; in this way, we could get through fourteen to sixteen members a day, starting at 8 am and finishing at 6 pm with an hour for lunch. Thirty-two members per weekend.

Other members of the club trap on a voluntary basis and generally help with clays, collecting empty cartridge cases and so on. The cost per member is fixed at 50p ($1.28) and any difference in the total is made up by the club.

Joe Wheater, a regular member of the England team, has also been to coach us. He has his own methods; he *shows* you how to shoot, and he makes it look easy. We have all learnt a great deal from him, and as a result of the coaching by these two experts, our shooting has improved out of all knowledge.

To encourage youngsters to take up the sport, we try to include a number of schoolboys among those to be coached by Rex Gage. We have also organised schoolboys' matches, and we have a Schoolboy Cup to be competed for. Under the spur of competition, the standard is extremely high, and we now have to make the competition difficult. We considered that the very young, armed with a .410, would need a plus handicap to even them up with their 'bigger' competitors. Never again! Most of the .410 shots were getting over the 'possible', when the handicap was added in.

Club Days: In the summer, we shoot on two evenings a week. Wednesday is 'club night'; one of the members works out the programme, and there is usually a small sweepstake. The 'duty officer' rigs all the traps, as well as supervising the scoring and trapping and so on; the whole evening is his responsibility. On Thursdays there is a Coaching Evening, when anybody can come up to be taught, or to practise a shot difficult to him. In the winter, we have the same programme on Sundays – with morning and afternoon sessions.

My advice, then, is that if you cannot start a club of your own – join one! It will make shooting much easier for you.

Then and now

I have always thought that the Edwardian era was the age when sporting shooting achieved its highest point. There was a good deal of shooting available; the rich had infinite leisure in which to shoot, and practically an infinite income on which to indulge it. The not so rich seldom had enough money to shoot at all. Thus, in general, shoots tended to get bigger and better, those who shot got more of it and so sometimes became more skilled.

Indeed, there arose several men who became such good shots that they were in great demand by those who had a shoot to 'establish' (and by gamekeepers who wanted a good bag to establish *them*). There are many stories of their prowess.

Lord Walsingham and Lord Ripon were once next to each other at a drive waiting for the pheasants to come. Suddenly a covey of eight partridges flicked over the hedge between them. They got the lot! This story was told at the time, not to emphasise what good shots they were, but to explain how skilful they were to know which bird was theirs and which that of their neighbour. I have a feeling that most of us, together with any neighbour we liked to name, would be lucky if we got more than three between us.

It is frequently said to me that people who 'shoot as much as that' ought to be good. But grouse flew no differently in those days, partridges no slower, and pheasants certainly no lower – in fact, almost certainly higher where that could be contrived. So their shooting technique must have been perfect, and if they could do it, certainly so can we.

The fact is that the good shot in the Edwardian era was very good indeed, and largely because most of them had a great deal of the best kind of practice at shooting game – which is to shoot game. But the average shot of those days was almost certainly of a lower standard.

What everybody lacked was anyone to teach them. Books on the subject were pretty hopeless; those who could shoot well did not know how they did it, certainly could not impart what knowledge they had, and were not particularly anxious to do so anyway. Thus those who could not shoot well and who were the least articulate, were told to teach the young idea. The keeper was given the job of instruction.

I once spent a long time with a keeper, and I learnt a very great deal – not least what a great man he was. (I wonder if employers realise what good service they got – and still get – from their keepers: and if they do, whether they do not take it rather too much for granted.) But that keeper did not teach me to shoot. He could not. To start with, any skill he possessed was virtually confined to shooting ground vermin – on the ground. I do not suppose he could have hit one bird in ten up in the air. When I missed, he did not know where I had missed, and certainly not why. His job really boiled down to giving a young boy opportunity to shoot at rabbits or pigeon. I learnt a lot about field craft and the country, but I did not learn how to shoot correctly. And this was how practically all present-day, keen, middle-aged shots 'learnt' to shoot. It was almost a fluke if they learnt the correct way.

It is different today. With clay pigeon clubs there is opportunity for intensive practice; often under skilled supervision. If you practise under

Coaching, with walkie-talkie for signalling to puller. This beginner is trying to *aim*, and trying too hard; not enough of the push of the gun towards the target

A good shot shows how: gun pointed at the target throughout mounting, snugly into the shoulder, triggers about to be pressed. He *looks* as if he will hit!

such conditions – in short if you are keen enough – you cannot fail to become a good shot; probably a very good shot. I am, of course, referring to sporting clays as opposed to Down the Line, though both can help. Indeed, I believe that among the best sporting shots in the country today is the good shot at sporting clays in an enthusiastic clay pigeon club. Seldom, if ever, does he get an opportunity to show his skill at really difficult driven pheasants and grouse. But put him in a first-class shoot, calm his nerves by telling him that the man with the Rolls-Royce and the pair of Purdeys probably has all his goods in the shop window, and he will outshoot everybody.

Perhaps another reason for the average standard of Edwardian shooting being rather lower than today was the inclination of the guns, in some cases, to do themselves rather too well. I have two photographs to illustrate this.

One photograph shows the guns at lunch outdoors and was obviously taken near the shoot. Beside the seated guns is a string orchestra of perhaps half-a-dozen players, the double bass looking particularly out of place in the open air. Although this may seem a bit odd, it is probably no worse than the transistor radio of today which, in my opinion, is equally out of place on the shooting field.

The other photograph shows a gun with about twenty pheasants in the air. Behind him are two loaders and a boy. There is nothing particularly odd about this, but there is one further feature in the picture which strikes me as rather splendid, or the opposite, whichever way you look at it. On the ground to the left rear of the gun (clear of the loaders) is spread a cloth; on the cloth are three champagne bottles – two on their sides empty, and one full. Closer examination suggests that the gentleman's footwork seems bereft of that easy fluency which no doubt characterised anyone who was good enough to shoot with three guns.

To sum up between 'Now' and 'Then', it can be said that shooting skill is *on the whole* better than it used to be, but still far below what could be achieved. A really good shot should kill and pick *consistently* more than he shoots at. And this without choosing his shots. Or put another way (if you feel that 'percentage kills' is a bad way to judge a man's shooting), he should kill a great deal more than he does today. The Edwardian experts showed what can be done; and if it could be achieved then, there are greater opportunities now for more people to achieve that very high standard.

There used to be a saying in those days about shooting a pheasant – 'Up gets a guinea, bang goes a penny-halfpenny, and down comes half-a-crown'. Which suggests that some costs were little different from ours, since I doubt if it costs a guinea to rear a pheasant even today. But guns were a different matter, and the Edwardian era produced the best shot guns ever made – certainly in terms of value for money. A best London gun cost about £65 ($160). A good example today of such a gun (although seventy years old), might cost ten times this amount; and it would be bought as a best gun to be used, and not for its 'antiquity' value. In other words, a best gun seventy years old would certainly compete with modern guns as to refinements, such as single trigger, ejection, easy opening and so on, and most certainly with regard to workmanship. But also if it had been reasonably looked after, it could compare in longevity, even though it would have to give seventy years start in this respect to its modern rivals.

There was intense competition to build a best gun, and I think there has been little improvement mechanically or in basic design since those days. This perfection was achieved, and at such a low price, because the craftsman engaged on such guns was a man of great integrity, dedicated to his work and unstinting in the skill he applied to it. I can think of no other mechanical contrivance designed seventy years ago which can compete with its modern counterpart. So to say that a best gun *built* seventy years can be very nearly as good a gun to use as its modern counterpart, is tribute indeed to the excellence of design and workmanship that was achieved. Get hold of such a gun, and you will see what I mean.

Equally, to say that a modern best gun is as good – or perhaps better – than an Edwardian 'best', is to give the highest praise possible to the modern best gun. In these days when mass-produced goods can be bought so cheaply – very often *must* be bought – there could be a strong temptation for even the best gunmakers to skimp somewhere. The saving in expensive labour would be great. But there is no skimping. Pride in craftsmanship still endures, perfection is still the ever-elusive goal, and the result is still beautiful.

4 Guns and Cartridges

Pattern and killing power

'Pattern fails before Penetration.' This is a nice slick phrase which, spoken quickly, does not mean much to most people. The word 'penetration' is of course strictly inaccurate, and perhaps a better term would be 'killing power' or 'blow'.

What is really meant is that, *on average*, by the time the pattern thrown by a shot gun fails, ie, there are large enough gaps for the bird to fly through unharmed, the shot itself will still have enough velocity and weight to kill. Put another way, after the pattern has failed, killing depends on luck.

Clearly, a gun firing dust shot would theoretically maintain its pattern beyond the point where the shot would kill. In such a case, the 'penetration' fails before 'pattern'. But I repeat, *on average,* it is the other way round.

Can we not get pattern and penetration (killing power) to fail together, and so get the best of both worlds?

We can, and there are two ways of doing it:

(a) Keep the shot closer together, or

(b) Use smaller shot, and so get more pellets.

I am assuming, for the moment, a constant velocity with a constant load.

We all know that keeping the shot closer together can be done by choking the gun, and this is indeed done. By a judicious selection of choke, the pattern can often (but by no means always) be held tight enough so that killing power and pattern will fail at about the same range. We can now select our size of shot, and work it out.

I must at this stage take some figures, which I will ask you to accept as virtually proven. They can be checked by reference to various text-books, notably those written by Burrard and Gough Thomas. They are shown as Tables 1–4 inclusive in Appendix II (Pattern and Killing Power, p 117).

Game Birds

First, let us assume that an average game bird – from pheasant to partridge or pigeon – requires, in order to be killed, to be hit by three pellets, each still carrying an energy of 0.86ft lb. To achieve this requires a pattern containing between 120 and 130 pellets in a 30in circle. (See Table 1 of Appendix II.)

Now, first, let us see at what range various sizes of shot still have 0.86ft lb left. Table 3 in the appendix shows that Nos 4 and 5 shot have plenty of energy at over 60yd, No 6 shot 'fails' at 55yd, and No 7 shot at 45yd. So much for the Penetration side of the problem.

Now let us see how difficult it is to get 120 to 130 pellets into a 30in circle at the Fail Penetration Range.

Let us assume $1\frac{1}{16}$oz shot as standard; then, knowing the number of shot in the cartridge, we can easily calculate the percentage of the pattern to meet the 130 requirements in the 30in circle. For instance, in $1\frac{1}{16}$oz of No 7 shot there are 361 pellets. The percentage of the pattern to meet our requirements is thus 130/361 or 36 per cent. It will be a higher percentage for larger shot. No 4 shot with half the pellets will require 72 per cent of the pattern in the 30in circle.

Now let us see what barrel boring will give this (and other percentages for different sized shot) at the Fail Penetration Range. These are:

Shot size	% in 30in circle to ensure pattern OK	Range where 'blow' fails	Boring, which will give percentage pattern at range
7	36%	45yd	True cylinder
6	45%	55yd	Full choke
5	56%	over 60yd	Not possible
4	72%	over 60yd	Not possible

(See Table 2 of Appendix II)

From the above, we see that:

(a) Big shot means fewer pellets, and *so it becomes more difficult to maintain pattern.*

(b) No 7 shot is sufficient against all medium game birds (including pigeon!) up to 45yd.

(c) We can at the same time afford to use an open bored gun, which will obviously make it easier to shoot well.

(d) Any bigger shot may (but may not!), give an increase in range: and then only at a price.

Let us now examine what bigger shot will achieve, and at what cost.

Suppose we insist on a killing range of 50yd. (Surely this is foolish, but go on!)

(a) No 7 shot: will not kill.

(b) No 6 shot: because there are fewer pellets, we have to insist on 45 per cent of the shot charge to ensure a good enough pattern. At 50yd, this can be achieved by three-quarters choke. (See Table 2 of Appendix II.)

But, since reducing the spread of the shot makes it harder to shoot well, to do so unnecessarily is obviously foolish. In actual fact, the spread of a true cylinder is roughly twice that thrown by three-quarters choke; (true at short ranges, and not quite so accurate at longer ranges).

We are thus clearly making it much more difficult for ourselves to shoot well (twice as difficult at short ranges), solely to increase our effective range from 45 to 50yd.

(c) No 5 shot: due to the yet smaller total number of pellets, we have to increase our percentage in a 30in circle to 56 per cent. Even with full choke, this can only be achieved at slightly over 45yd.

The loss of spread is even more severe with a full choke compared with a three-quarters choke and No 6 shot (above). In fact, the spread is now less than half that of a true cylinder and we have gained virtually nothing in effective range. We have made it twice as hard for ourselves, for no gain at all.

(d) No 4 shot: still fewer pellets in the total charge. Therefore we have to raise the percentage of the total charge into a 30in circle to 72 per cent. With a full choke, this is just about possible at 40yd. Thus we have to depend upon a really tight pattern which makes it yet harder for you to shoot well, *and* involves a reduction in effective range.

These results are so illuminating that it is worth seeing what happens with other birds, both larger and smaller.

Duck and Hare

We will assume as follows:

Hare and duck require (to be killed) three pellets each of 1.0ft lb; and 100 pellets in a 30in circle to ensure that the pattern is sufficiently dense. Then the following table gives the true picture:

Size of Shot	Percentage Pattern required to kill	Penetration Fail Range	Boring of Gun to achieve this
7 Shot	28%	40/50yd*	True cylinder
6 Shot	35%	50yd	Imp. cylinder
5 Shot	43%	55yd	Full choke
4 Shot	55%	Over 60yd	Not possible

* 'Blow' fails at 40yd. Pattern good up to 50

Thus for the heavy bird, we can see that:

(a) No 7 shot: good and advantageous out to 40yd. You are getting the maximum chance of hitting due to the large spread of a true cylinder.

(b) No 6 shot: using an improved cylinder, is almost ideal. Effective to 50yd.

(c) No 5 shot: if you can accept 50yd as a maximum range, you can get away with half or perhaps three-quarters choke. This is definitely less value than No 6 shot, because we have the same effective range, and a tighter spread.

(d) No 4 shot: to achieve our 55 per cent pattern, we require a three-quarters choke which will only be effective to 45yd. (Full choke will not manage a good enough pattern at 50yd.) We thus lose 5yd in range without any compensating advantage.

Snipe

Let us now examine the smaller bird such as a snipe. To kill such a bird we require a blow of 0.5ft lb per pellet. Two pellets are sufficient, and the minimum pattern required is 270.

Then table is then as follows:

Shot	% of Pattern	Range of 'blow' failure	Boring
7	$77\frac{1}{2}$%	60yd	Not possible even with full choke
6	100%	Over 60yd	,,
5	100%	,,	,,
4	100%	,,	,,

It is thus evident that, even with No 7 shot, we have not enough pellets, but have too much energy. We *must* therefore use No 8 or even No 9 shot against snipe.

Conclusions

The conclusions are inescapable. Basically, we are going to get the best results by reducing the size of the shot and thus getting more pellets; and opening the bore of the gun, and thus (incidentally) making it easier for ourselves to shoot well.

We can prove this because we can see that for normal game shooting:

(a) No 7 shot and a true cylinder are best for 'medium' game.

(b) No 6 shot and improved cylinder are best for duck and hare.

(c) No 7 shot is actually too big for snipe.

(d) Any form of choke (other than improved cylinder) is no advantage whatever. It is a disadvantage.

(e) Any shot larger than No 6 is disadvantageous.

To tighten the pattern and use heavier shot will almost certainly make it more difficult for ourselves, or actually reduce the effective range – or both!

And is not this borne out in practice? When we ask someone how he got on after the drive, how often do we hear him say, 'Quite well, but I missed one or two "sitters" I ought to have had'. Exactly! If he had an open-bored gun he would have got them as well.

You just do not fire at game over 50yd – seldom that. Why then handicap yourself with closely-bored guns which make it more difficult for you; and big shot which reduces the effective range? And in passing, why buy high-velocity loads; you are merely adding to the 'blow' which is too big anyway, and probably reducing the pattern in the process!

Commonsense might suggest that to increase the power of your gun, you should employ heavier shot, driven faster. I have shown that this is wrong. It is like the story of the Young Bull and the Old Bull talking together.

'Let's dash down and do one of them Cows', says the Young Bull.

'No', says the Old Bull, 'Let's *walk* down, and do the lot!'

If you insist on high velocity and big shot, the cartridge-maker will sell them to you. If, on the other hand, you can get a cartridge with *more* shot you will do better. If you have your gun bored out as well, you will do better still!

They knew this eighty years ago. Lord Walsingham, who on one occasion in 1888 shot 1,056 grouse by himself in one day, always used nothing but cylinder-bored guns. If he found it paid to make it as easy as possible for himself, why should we not follow suit?

I do; I always shoot with No 7 shot in 25-in barrels, bored full cylinder and improved cylinder. And if I hold straight, down they come!

How to choose your first gun

This is a most difficult section to write since so much depends on your physical measurements, your age, how keen you are, what you expect to shoot and, last but by no means least, the depth of your pocket.

Perhaps the most important factor is how keen you are. If you have done a little shooting but are still not quite sure that you are going to enjoy it, you should not spend too much on any gun. Here, however, I am going to assume that the bug has really bitten you and that you want the best gun you can afford.

Under 18s and Over 60s

If you are between eighteen and sixty years of age, you will probably be physically big and strong enough to handle most guns. Outside these limits, there are likely to be those who may find difficulty in handling the weight of the average gun. For such people, only the 20-bore, 16-bore and 12-bore 'light' guns need be considered. There are guns in other bores, but they have no material advantages over 20, 16 or 12; in fact, several disadvantages.

The 20-bore weighs between $5\frac{1}{4}$ to $5\frac{3}{4}$lb; the 16, $5\frac{1}{2}$–6lb and the 'light' 12-bore, $5\frac{3}{4}$ to $6\frac{1}{4}$lb. Virtually the only limitation which lack of years, or excess of them imposes, is on the weight of gun that can easily be carried. Lack of weight in a gun imposes also one limitation on the firer, and that is the quantity of shot (ie, the shot load) that can be fired at a time. It might just be possible in exceptional circumstances to get a 20-bore to fire a full 12-bore load of shot, if you chambered the gun suitably and got a special cartridge.

A 12-bore gun weighing say, 7lb could absorb the opposite and equal reaction of pushing out over an ounce of shot at a normal velocity, without bruising your shoulder. A 20-bore weighing, say, 5lb would not. The effect on the shooter in such a case, would be disastrous. The lighter gun – whatever its bore – is thus limited as to the charge of shot that it can fire, and is limited in this purely by the inability of the firer to absorb the recoil.

It is not always known that the spread (from similar choked barrels and at similar ranges) of a 20-, 16- and 12-bore is the same. If there are fewer number of shot in a 20-bore cartridge (as there must be), our *pattern* is going to fail earlier. (This applies to a lesser degree to the 16, and lesser still to a light 12-bore). In other words, the effective range of these guns is less than the 'standard' 12-bore.

It will not be reduced very much. In fact if you use No 7 shot and full cylinder, you have a 20-bore effective against medium game (pigeons, partridges, pheasants etc,) up to 37yd, and better than that of course for the 16-bore, and better still for the light 12-bore.

This seems a very small price to pay for being able to handle your gun easily. True that the lighter the gun, the greater the loss of range you will have to accept, but in actual practice this will not amount to very much.

You could, of course, make up this loss of range a bit by choking your gun. You will get a bit of range back, and you will lose a lot of spread which will make your shooting more difficult. I know which way I would prefer to have it.

Type of Gun

Now as to the type of gun for the under 18s and over 60s. Since you are limited in weight, the gun must be either a single barrel, or a side by side double. You will not wish to pay a lot of money for the under-18 boy, even if there are a lot of younger brothers 'coming on', so a single barrel is a possibility here. But single barrel guns are often comparatively clumsy weapons. If you can afford it, I would suggest basically a double-barrel hammerless gun.

As for the over 60s, my firm advice is to get the best gun you can afford. A best London gun will cost the earth – and is worth it, as must be any object which has been so meticulously fashioned for long hours by such skilled hands. It will cost you the same whether it is a 12-bore, a 'light' 12-, 16- or 20-bore (or even a .410, for that matter). It will last you, your son, and his son (and longer), if reasonably looked after. It will handle and function beautifully. It will appreciate in value. Having whetted your appetite, I will not spoil it by telling you the cost. If you must, find out. Give your gasp of disbelief, and then read on.

So far, we have narrowed the choice to a double-barrelled gun of a weight that can be conveniently carried and handled. For the people we are considering at the moment, this must hold good irrespective of what one intends to shoot. Broadly speaking, the cost of the guns we are considering will be the same whether they are .410s or 12-bore or anything in between. Our problem is thus easier now that we have decided on the weight and type of gun; the choice will depend solely on cost. As always, you have to pay for what you get. So let us see what we can do without, if we must.

Sidelock or Box Lock: Box lock is cheaper and a bit lighter. It is perhaps marginally inferior in a number of ways compared to a sidelock; but on balance for what we are considering, it will save money to go for a box lock – all else being equal.

Single or Double Trigger: The single trigger is complicated, expensive and basically less reliable. There is, for a beginner not much advantage. Therefore, double trigger.

Ejector or Non-Ejector: All guns have what is known as primary ejection; that is the cartridge, whether fired or not, is lifted clear of the breech when the gun is opened, so that it can be easily lifted out with the fingers. An ejector gun ejects the fired cartridge (and only the fired one) clear of the gun, when the gun is opened. It is thus quicker and more easy to reload.

Do you really want an ejector? They add greatly to the cost, and to the complication, and in the cheaper gun complication may cause a loss of reliability.

Engraving: If you wish to save money, avoid engraving which is expensive; it will not help you to kill a bird.

New or Second-Hand: A good English second-hand gun may well prove a bargain. It may be possible to pick up a pedigree non-ejector, for example, at a very reasonable price. But there are snags in the second-hand market of guns, in the same way as there are snags in the second-hand motorcar market. Remember, too, that we are at this stage considering 'light 12's, 16-, 20-bore or .410s only. The number of these on the second-hand market is limited.

Your sources, therefore, are:

(a) The reputable dealer, from whom the good second-hand gun can never be cheap.

(b) Friends who have boys' or 'family' light guns available, and on whom you can rely.

(c) Buying a second-hand gun from advertised sources.

This means, ideally, seeking the help of a really knowledgeable friend.

In short, you just may be able to get a really good gun well suited to you at a reasonable price on the second-hand market. But, as a beginner, you are more likely to get something less than ideal for *you*.

New Guns: There are several makers, both English and foreign, who make good guns well below the top price. Many of them make 16- and 20-bore guns, which will come within your 'weight of gun' category. You can probably rule out the 'light 12' which has to be carefully designed to achieve a light weight, and is therefore expensive.

You will be buying a comparatively mass-produced article – indeed like the average car – which will take a bit of running in, and conceivably may develop initially a minor fault or two (which can easily be put right).

It is possible to buy a foreign gun 'in the white' – that is, in its basic condition made with very good materials; and then subsequently to have it 'tuned up' to your requirements. By tuning up, I mean having it passed for British Proof, stock fitted to your measurements, barrels blued and so on. To give some idea of the costs involved, the price of the gun itself in the white might be about £100. To have the gun fully 'tuned up', engraved and so on, would cost a further £150.

You can buy a foreign double-barrelled gun for less than this, but the above will give you an idea of how little can be devoted to the 'tuning up' of any gun, if it is not to cost a good deal.

Summary: For the under 18s and over 60s: get yourself a double-barrelled side-by-side gun with two triggers, of a bore (and thus weight), to suit you. To save money, go for a box lock and non-ejector – no engraving. It should, I think, be new, and can be of a foreign imported make. Within the limitations I have suggested, pay as much as you can. You will not be disappointed. There is one proviso for the over 60s. Pick up, handle and if possible shoot a 'best' gun to see what it is like. If you can afford it, buy it. You have after all only about thirty years left in which to enjoy it, and this is only just long enough to get the full pleasure and enjoyment that such a lovely thing is able to give you during that time.

What will you have if you buy a new gun of the type I have recommended, probably for under £100 ($250.00), or maybe less than half this sum?

The disadvantages will be that the gun will be:

(a) Rather stiff to open and close and operate initially.
(b) Somewhat clumsy by comparison with what can be achieved by expensive weapons.
(c) Almost certainly too heavily choked in both barrels.
(d) Stock not fitted to your measurements, which is not too important.

You will have a gun:

(a) Which will be to your weight.
(b) Will be a good killer.
(c) Will prove basically reliable.
(d) Within its known limitations, will do what you want and will give you pleasure.

Guns for the Average Man

So far we have considered only those people whose choice of weapon is limited by the weight they can reasonably carry around. For the average man, between the ages of eighteen and sixty, this weight factor is not nearly so important, and so a wider choice becomes available. We can also take into closer account the type of shooting for which it is required, and this can be separated into four categories.

(a) Wildfowl shooting.
(b) Game and rough shooting.
(c) Down the Line clay pigeon shooting.
(d) Skeet shooting.

Ideally, a different gun will be best for each category, but do not be alarmed as, in practice, one gun will be pretty well all right for all four categories. But if you are going to concentrate on one type of shooting, then one type of gun will suit you better.

Wildfowl: Most duck are heavy birds requiring a heavy shot blow. Duck are also very wary and so one tends to have to shoot at long ranges. Both these factors often call for a gun heavy enough to throw a heavy load of shot. It may thus be thought desirable to have a 12-bore gun chambered for 3in cartridges which will contain a large number of pellets.

Do not get a gun that is (a) too heavily choked, or, (b) too heavy. Both these factors may make it too difficult to shoot well. And remember, you will sometimes want to use your gun against rabbits, pigeons and perhaps game. Let me repeat, for it is all-important: *do not get a gun too heavy, or too heavily choked.*

I would suggest a double-barrelled 12-bore, $2\frac{3}{4}$ chambers, improved cylinder and half-choke, two triggers and perhaps ejector. As good as you can afford. Weight not more than $7\frac{1}{4}$lb, preferably less; if you are really determined, a similar weapon but with 3in chambers and inevitably a bit heavier. If you buy this latter weapon and accept more choke (as everyone will advise you), you will no doubt *think* that you will kill more duck, but you will bag fewer.

I have not recommended an 'Under and Over', nor a 'Pump' gun. I believe the place for both these guns is in the clay pigeon field. But see later.

Game and Rough Shooting: What has already been said about the under 18s and over 60s applies here. The gun I would recommend would be a 12-bore hammerless ejector with two triggers and 'straight' grip. Weight about 6½lb, 2½in chambers, and bored full cylinder and improved cylinder. As expensive as you can afford.

To take the last point first. The more you pay, the more you will get. If you pay a lot for your gun, you will have a weapon that will be a joy to look at, and certainly a great pleasure to handle. It will function in a most immaculate way, the trigger pulls will be crisp and of the correct weight, the ejection will be identical for each barrel and strong, the gun will be easy to open whether fired or not, and close, and every piece of the mechanism will work like silk. It will throw a pattern for which it has been designed every time, and it will last.

Finally, it will have a natural 'pointability'. This is difficult to describe, but very easy to appreciate when you have such a gun in your hands. Some makers seem to have the knack of achieving this – and some have not. The fact remains that a 'best' gunmaker can achieve a gun that 'feels' wonderful. It will be 'sympathetic' when you are shooting badly; it will rejoice with you when you are shooting well. You will, in short, shoot better in spite of yourself.

Pointability: I believe part of the answer is in the designer achieving most of the weight of the gun in the centre of the gun so that it is concentrated more between the hands when you are mounting.

Suppose for a matter of argument, a 12-bore gun weighing 6½lb could be made with fibreglass barrels and fibreglass butt, both of feather weight. Then it is obvious that you would be handling a weapon with virtually all the weight between your hands, and it would be almost as easy to point as your own finger. And it is the improving skill of gunmakers that is getting nearer to this. Even so, I do not believe it is the absolute ideal for which we should aim. A highly 'pointable' gun is all right so far as it goes, but it may lack stability and momentum.

And by stability I mean the ability of the gun to keep ON the target. If it gets ON quickly, it may also tend to get OFF quickly. By momentum, I mean the ability of the gun to help the swing to keep going. There is certainly one high class maker's guns seem to me 'nose heavy'; and though I am sure this was designed in, I find them sulky to point.

Length of Barrel: Men who shoot are conservative people, and it takes a long time to change ideas, or perhaps prejudices. Up to the end of the nineteenth century, black powder (gunpowder) was used as a propellant in cartridges. Gunpowder had many assets as a propellant; probably the most advantageous was that it gave the charge of shot a comparatively slow push out of the barrel. You can *hear* this, if you go to a Game Fair and watch the 'old fashioned shooters' firing at clays with black powder and muzzle loaders. This slow push required a comparatively long barrel – 32 inches was probably ideal – to enable the slow-burning propellant to develop sufficient muzzle velocity.

When the modern quick-burning propellants came in, it took about forty years to realise that a long barrel was no longer necessary. It was Churchill who first introduced the 25in barrel and its advent was marked by a long drawn and fierce fight – between the XXV School, and the 30in barrel advocates. Now that the dust of this controversy has subsided a bit, we can perhaps look at it all in a more objective way.

First, we can take it as fact that the reduction in muzzle velocity developed by a 25in barrel compared with, say, a 30in barrel is negligible. It is there, admittedly, but is so small that it can be ignored. It may also be accepted that there is no deterioration in pattern produced, solely due to the different lengths of barrel. Finally, with a raised rib, both barrels *seem* the same length when you are shooting.

What then are the advantages and disadvantages of the short barrel length over the longer 'normal' barrel?

(a) The shorter barrel enables more weight to be concentrated in the centre of the gun, and therefore it becomes more 'pointable'.
(b) The gun can be made lighter.
(c) It is at present fashionable!

The disadvantages are that, with a big man with long arms, the stock becomes long and the gun with short barrels then looks out of proportion. This is not quite such a silly argument as it may seem. Whatever it is, a thing must look right to be right. A ship is a very typical example; a building, too. And, nearer home, a pretty girl.

The ease of pointability of a gun probably matters less to a big strong man, and so he can take advantage of the increased momentum and increased stability of the longer barrel.

In brief, I believe that the short-barrelled gun has advantages for most of us. On the other hand, when I am lucky enough to shoot with two guns, I cannot tell in a hot corner whether I have got my 25in barrelled gun, or the 28in in my hand.

Summing Up: For game and rough shooting I would recommend a 12-bore side-by-side double-barrel gun, bored full cylinder and improved cylinder, weighing not more than 6½lb. I would suggest short barrels.

According to the depth of your pocket, you may also be able to afford ejectors. If you can pay more, you can get also the inbuilt workmanship and pointability of a hand-built gun.

Clay Shooting: There are two basic types of clay shooting. Down the Line and skeet (and sporting) shooting and each sport really requires a different type of gun if you are going to concentrate on it.

Down the Line: The most usual type of gun used by the best shots at Down the Line shooting is the 'Under and Over'. The reason for this is the ease with which a 'single' barrel enables one to get 'on' to the clay. And this is an overwhelming advantage.

True that there are also some disadvantages in an 'Under and Over', and these may be summarised as: (a) they are heavy; (b) they are comparatively clumsy; and, (c) they require the gun to open through a big angle to enable the lower barrel to be loaded.

These disadvantages are apparent in game and rough shooting, but do not matter at all in Down the Line shooting; in fact, the heaviness may be a positive help on occasion.

Since you are firing at an end-on clay target at longish ranges, pattern is everything. To this end, plenty of small shot is used (the heavy gun helps to reduce the recoil felt by the shooter), and both barrels are heavily choked. (Since 'blow' needed is small, and close ranges never used, choke at last becomes advantageous). In addition, the rib on the top of the barrel is raised and ventilated, so that when the gun gets hot, the cool rib will not heat the air above it and so 'bend' the line of sight between gun and clay. Handling and pointability do not particularly matter, since the gun is mounted to the shoulder before the clay is called.

I believe that the 'Under and Over' *could* also be a very successful game gun, and it is even possible that the disadvantage of having to have a wide opening could be overcome by allowing the gun to open sideways. At least two makers have produced an elegant and not too heavy 'Under and Over', although they are expensive.

An alternative to the 'Under and Over' is the automatic gun, which has a single barrel and therefore a big advantage for Down the Line shooting. Again, it is heavy, comparatively clumsy and difficult to load quickly. But it is often possible to get varying degrees of choke in the form of an adaptor. These adaptors can be screwed on to the end of the barrel, and thus the gun becomes more flexible to use than the true 'Under and Over' Down the Line gun. It can certainly be used for rough shooting and wildfowl, but is not suitable for game shooting in large numbers.

Skeet Shooting: This shooting is done at short ranges. All that has been written about game guns applies here, except that since there is virtually no need to fire at over thirty yards, the gun to use ideally requires full cylinder boring, and short barrels to achieve quick pointing. I would not be surprised if, one day, guns specifically intended for skeet shooting were bored slightly 'bell mouthed', on the lines of the old blunderbuss, solely to increase the spread.

Buying the Gun: Talk to your friends. Get as much advice as you can; gradually your need will clarify, and you will get a clear picture of what you want.

Go to your local gunmaker and talk to him; handle as many guns as you can. Do not be influenced by fancy engraving. Finally, put a limit on the price you are prepared to pay and stick to it.

If there is a clay pigeon club in your neighbourhood, ask if you may visit it. Most clubs will usually welcome someone who will work the traps. It will not be long before the members are showing you their guns and you will be able to feel and compare them for yourself.

Introducing a boy to shooting

The best age for a young boy to start shooting depends pretty well entirely on two factors: his keenness and his physical strength and size.

A young boy who is not desperately keen on 'having a go', or to start shooting, is frankly at a disadvantage if he has to start shooting with a .410. It is relatively difficult to hit a moving target with the small spread given by such a small gun, and success is all-important at this early stage. In such a case, it might perhaps be better to keep what interest there is simmering until he is physically big enough to handle a 20-bore. In short, a young boy has got to be keen. And, probably just as important, he has to be given great encouragement at once.

The other factor is physical size and strength. A boy of eleven can usually handle a .410. But even then, a small boy has a strong tendency to lean back to counter the comparatively large weight of the gun when he mounts it. Which, of course, is wrong.

So whatever you do, do not give him too big a gun too soon. Give him a 20-bore too early, and the recoil may give him a knock and frighten him. It may cause him to flinch, a habit which, if acquired at this stage, will last for a very long time. Do not risk it, whatever you do. Keep him on a little gun and encourage him by getting him to hit the clays. Obviously, at this stage he must only fire his gun under expert tuition. So get him firing it at moving targets with someone teaching who knows what he is about.

When he is big enough, put him on a bigger gun – always with the proviso that it must *under no circumstances* be too big from the mounting and recoil angle. With the bigger gun the target becomes easier to hit, and so he is given further encouragement.

If a boy is keen enough he will quickly overcome the inevitable disappointments and, given sound basic training and sufficient encouragement, he will reap a rich reward in later years.

First, he will never be a bad shot. (This would be a turn-up for most of us!). This is because he will find it comparatively difficult to learn bad habits, because the right habits will have become ingrained.

He will never revert to bad shooting habits in moments of stress – like the rest of us do – because he will never have had bad shooting habits.

When things go wrong, a small correction will put them right; it will not need the whole swing being taken to pieces and put together again.

He will have a firm foundation for ever, on which to build his skill.

Finally, a small boy can indeed attain considerable skill. Another true story. We have a very fast trap with an International arm on our high tower. It throws a fast bird that is about 25yd high. This *looks* very high indeed, so much so that one quite experienced shot, unable to hit them

A small boy has a strong tendency to lean back to counter the weight of the gun when he mounts it

with his 12-bore, maintained that they were out of shot.

His son, aged eleven and perfectly coached by a very experienced instructor, then hit ten running with his .410. After about the sixth hit, he turned round and said 'It's easy, Dad'. It was intense pleasure to watch perfection in miniature as displayed by this young boy. It was also worth seeing the expression on his father's face!

All guns, even for youngsters, are expensive, and not least a .410. Perhaps you may know of boys who are growing out of theirs and from whom you could buy. And extra expense may sometimes be justified if there are any younger brothers or friends to whom the gun, when it has been outgrown, can be passed on.

You can also save money by getting a single barrel, but do *not* get a bolt-action model or a hammer gun at this stage. Some of the bolt-action models are pigs to load, and to handle. Nor are hammer guns suitable for weak fingers and thumbs; they can be dangerous.

How a 'best' gun is built

In this age of mass-production a visit to the workshops of a leading British firm of gunmakers provides reassuring evidence that true craftsmanship – the loving, patient work of men highly skilled in the use of their hands and striving always for perfection – still flourishes in industry.

I was once privileged to visit the workshops of one such firm, Holland & Holland, Gunmakers Ltd, and the extent to which perfection is sought with every 'best' gun they produce was a revelation to me. Only twenty-five per cent of the work is done by machines, the rest is hand-made and fitted. This proportion has a commonsense angle to it; where a quarter of an inch of metal has to be removed, it is done (quickly) by a machine. Where only a 'thou' has to be taken off, it is done (more accurately) by hand.

Everything of a best gun is made at Holland & Holland except the rough barrel forgings, the locks, and the French walnut blanks for the stocks. All machined bits (metal or wood) come from the machine shop – the barrels roughly bored and shaped, the actions, locks, trigger, ejectors and so on – all in the rough. It is possibly an over-simplification to say that all 'bits' designed to fit *into* something, come from the machine shop

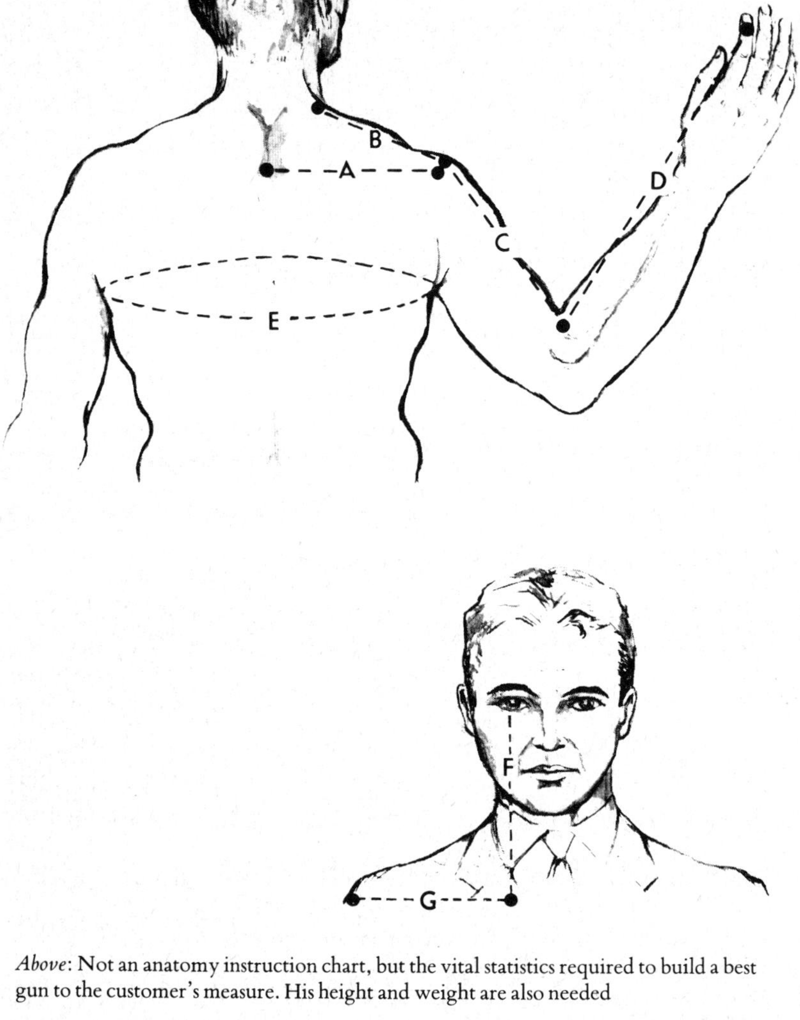

Above: Not an anatomy instruction chart, but the vital statistics required to build a best gun to the customer's measure. His height and weight are also needed

Opposite: The hand of the craftsman at work on a chequer-pattern for the stock of a Purdey gun. Stocks are cut from blocks of the very finest walnut

too big. Any bit designed to receive another part is machined out too small.

It is the job – or rather the jobs – of the action shop to fit the bits together. This is all done by hand, using the smoke method to ensure a perfect fit of every part. To take a simple example; the barrels have to be fitted to the action so that when the gun is closed there is a perfect fit between them. The barrel ends and lumps are held over a candle so that the metal which is to make contact with the action is slightly darkened by the smoke of the candle. The barrels are then fitted to the action and then taken off again. The smoke-darkened parts will then show light shiny patches where they made contact with the action, and these patches are removed with a very fine file. The whole process is then repeated until all the metal is evenly bright after the gun has been closed and opened. The tolerance is NIL; the fit is accurate to the size of a particle of smoke. All parts are fitted to each other in this manner, including the locks let in to the wooden stock.

All this takes time, patience and skill. For instance, it will take an average of seventeen hours to ensure the perfect fit and working of the safety catch; to fit the extractors to the barrels, slightly longer. But they fit at the end of it, $\pm$ NIL.

The barrels, before getting to the action shop, are brazed together and bored full choke in the barrel shop. Extreme care is taken to ensure that the two barrels are level and parallel. When the barrels have been fitted to the action, infinite patience is shown in ensuring that the hole bored in the action to take the striker is dead central with regard to the barrels. Thus if the cartridge is round and the percussion cap central (as it always is) the striker will hit the cap bang in the middle every time. (If you do not own a best gun, have a look at one of your fired cartridges; has the percussion cap been struck *dead* central? Or nearly; or even to one side!).

When the gun is roughly fitted together, all parts are then checked. This takes one man (who has worked at Holland & Holland for thirty-six years) eleven hours. Anything not perfect is corrected.

The stock is fitted to the gun in the stocking shop, and the customer will usually have chosen his stock of French walnut in the rough. It will take fifty-five hours to fit the stock to the gun and let in the locks, a further seventeen hours to shape the stock to the customer's measurements, and a yet further fifteen hours to polish it. The polishing is done by hand with linseed oil and a very fine abrasive, in much the same manner as one 'bones' a pair of shoes or boots.

The gun is now sent to the shooting school, where a regulator (a man who must indeed possess a peculiarly high degree of a peculiar skill) alters the degree, shape and practically every other dimension of the choke, to ensure that the gun always shoots to the percentage pattern specified by the customer.

The gun goes back to the engraving shop and is then engraved. This, of course, is all done by hand, and a 'standard' Holland & Holland engraving will take about seventy hours. An engraving of a special nature might take up to 400 hours. One of the engravers gave as an example of such an engraving, 'a picture of the owner's favourite dog chasing a pheasant'. It made me grin to find this small 'imperfection' amongst so much perfection.

The engravers say that they never stop learning, and they reckon it takes forty years experience to produce a really good engraver. I saw their practice plates. These are flat pieces of metal measuring about 5in × 2in and, originally, about $\frac{1}{4}$in thick. They are engraved with various 'parts' of standard designs, purely as practice. When completely covered, these engravings are rubbed off and the process repeated. The plates I saw were all paper thin. I asked how good an engraver was at the end of this. He said that he himself had then been allowed to engrave the head of one screw in a gun.

Finally the gun is passed to the finishing shop, where the gun is indeed finished. It is taken completely to pieces and the whole action regulated, trigger pulls adjusted and so on. This will take about seventy hours.

In spite of the extreme accuracy of fit and workmanship, there is so much individual work put into each gun that the character of the man who did that work becomes stamped on the gun itself. An expert at Holland & Holland can tell at once which men had fitted the various parts of any gun made in their workshop.

It will be two years from the date you place your order before you get your gun or guns. When you do get it, it will not look superficially very different from any other. But as soon as you handle it and use it, you will at once realise that this is no ordinary gun but the product of superlative

MADE IN
ENGLAND

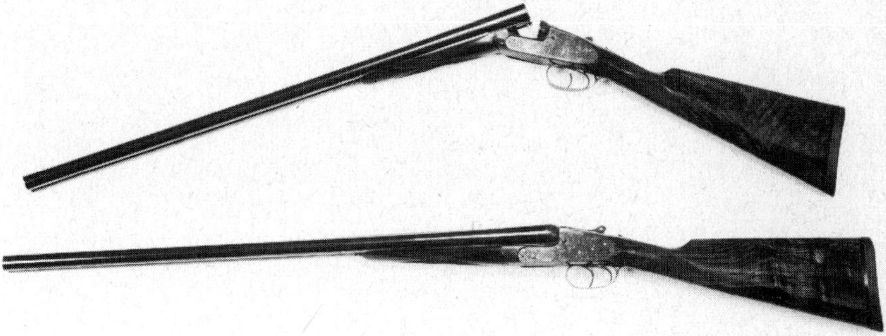

Broken and closed: a Purdey hammerless ejector. Note intricate engraving and the magnificent overall finish. Customers stipulate choice of barrel length and weight, and can order an extra pair of barrels with different bore and length

Clay pigeon shooting *de luxe*: a Purdey hammerless ejector trap gun, specially designed for the sport after meticulous observation at the traps, with the tough requirements of American Clay Bird Shooting in mind

Opposite: The rough stock takes shape at the Purdey works. The superb final finish is already well advanced and the craftsman is working on the recess for the decorated lockplate. Stocks have to be worked, hollowed and weighted exactly

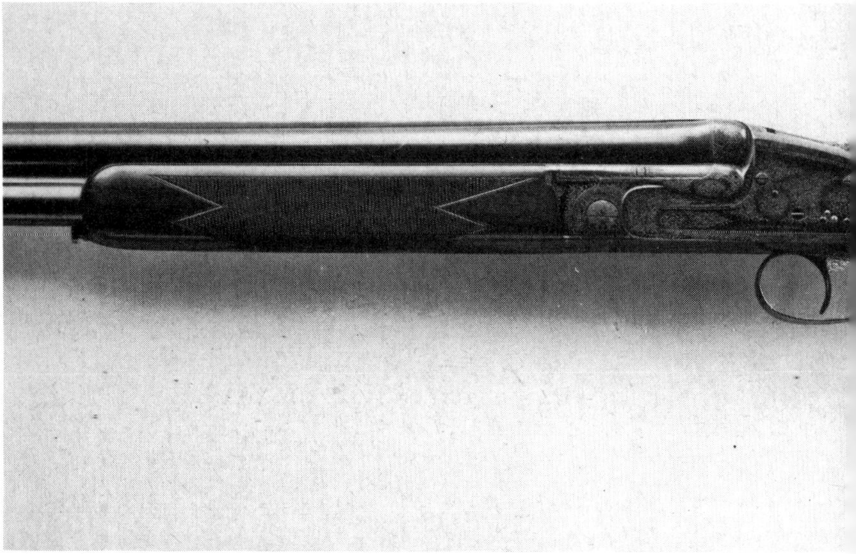

A Purdey 'Over and Under' Gun. With the distinctive vertical arrangement of its barrels, the 'Over and Under' gun was a response to the growing interest in clay bird shooting. It is suitable for game shooting, live pigeon and clay shooting

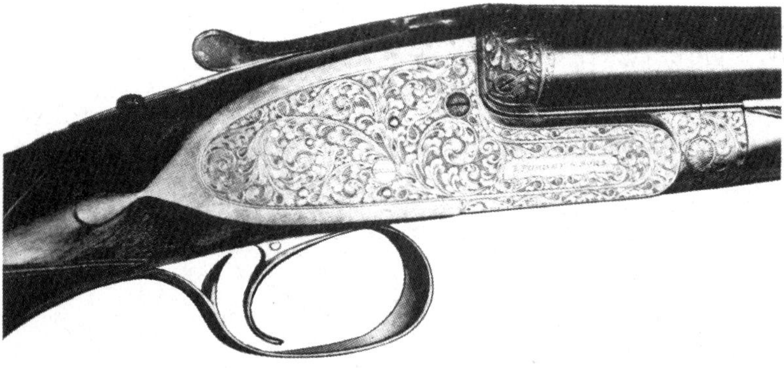

The gun as fine art: a Purdey extra finished gun. The lockplate has been given a flowing scroll decoration, and the breech of the gun is carved with oak leaves and acorns. As ever, the customer can stipulate the design he wants

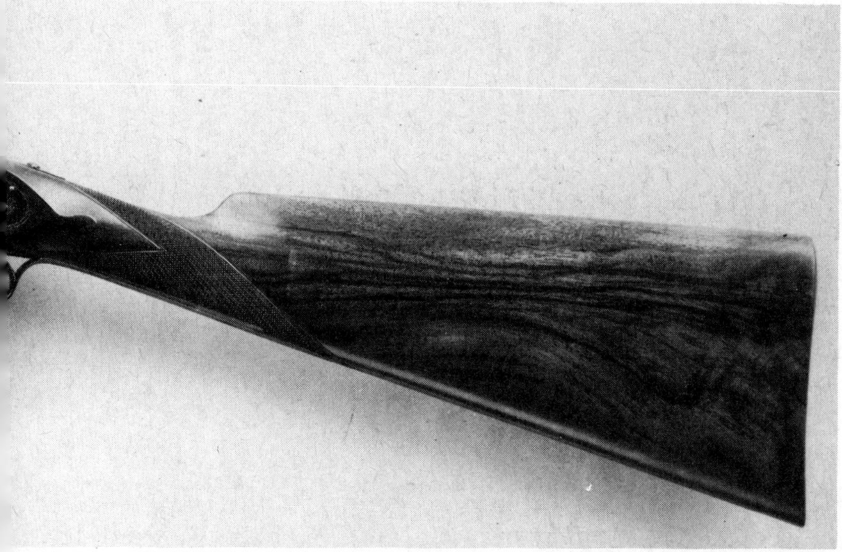

This is the standard Purdey fine engraving finish, included in the basic cost of the gun unless the customer prefers to order a special design of his own choosing. Note that the carving extends to the heads of the larger screws

skill laboriously acquired and applied to your weapon with care, patience and integrity. When you have paid for this, it will have cost a lot in pound notes; but you will have bought something pretty near priceless, dirt cheap.

There are other best gunmakers in London and other cities, and no doubt they produce weapons of a similar class and in a similar way to the method I have briefly described. They must produce very good weapons to stay in business; and most of them have been in business for a great number of years.

5 Behaviour When Shooting

You may kill, or you may miss
But at all times remember this,
All the pheasants ever bred
Won't repay for one man dead.

Safety

With a shot gun, you have a weapon in your hand which will not only kill a human being but which at close range is more lethal than an anti-tank rifle. Not only can it kill your friend, but it can kill you. At longer ranges it can wound or blind.

I am therefore going to divide safety drill up into two factors: *Handling*, which affects you and your friends close to; and *Firing*, which is more likely (though not necessarily) to affect your friends further away.

And remember as you read that you will not see yourself as ever likely to be dangerous. Very few people do anything deliberately with a gun that is unsafe. Or to put it another way, they always think they are safe. This applies to all of us.

Here, then, are some rules, and if you observe them all, and at all times, you will never have a shooting accident.

Handling

(a) When you get a gun into your hand OPEN IT to see if it is loaded. I can always tell the man who has done a bit of shooting; I hand him his gun, and see if he opens it. If he does, OK. If he does not, watch out! You must do it *always*. I am constantly opening my gun to make quite sure it is empty. I knew someone who was a safe gun. He was getting into a Land Rover after a drive, and for the fortieth time opened his gun purely from habit. He told me later that he knew it was empty. It was loaded! He has never forgotten it. Learn from his mistake.

Frequently we read of someone injured or killed 'cleaning his gun'. It just could not occur if a gun is always opened when picked up.

A line of beaters in action, advancing through a crop of kale. The bird they have just flushed will be a long way up by the time he reaches the trees!

(b) When not shooting – UNLOAD. This applies when talking with other people, or when by oneself. To make clear that you are unloaded, open the gun. Then everyone can see. To put the safety catch on is not enough. The safety catch only locks the triggers; the gun is still fully cocked. Before the gun ever leaves your hand – unload. Do not put it down for a moment, without unloading.

(c) Before you load for the first time, look through the barrels. There may be a bit of cleaning stuff left up the barrel; there may be a bit of snow (frozen into a lump of ice), flipped up your barrel from someone's heel, whilst you were walking behind him. Look through your barrels before shooting. If there is any blockage, your gun may burst on firing.

(d) Unload when climbing a gate or hedge. This applies particularly when by oneself, where you may think 'it does not matter'.

You cannot be too safe, and your gun is only completely safe when it is unloaded. If in doubt – unload. A council of perfection? Possibly, but you must achieve perfection in this – nothing less.

Firing

The rule is as simple as this: do not point your gun towards anyone. Of course! You never would. But it is very easy to do so, and you must be constantly on your guard.

Let us take some examples.

You are walking up when a bird gets up behind you, and you turn round and shoot it. Do you KNOW no-one was behind you – had perhaps stopped to pick up a bird?

The bird goes forward low and you fire. Is the hedge at the end of the field in range and anyone behind it? Do you KNOW?

The bird swings round right and you shoot. How close to your next-door gun or beater, or the man beyond slightly out of line? Not only must you not fire, but you must not point the gun at the bird. You are breaking the rule if you do!

I, as a young boy, was brought up with the knowledge that if I ever broke this rule and pointed my gun at anyone, I would be sent home. My cousin, aged about fourteen, and I were once asked by his father to shoot partridges for the first time. We both had been looking forward to this intensely for many weeks – a lifetime it seemed. It was a lovely day and

When not shooting—UNLOAD. This applies when talking with other people or when by oneself

With the guns. Main point to note is the perfect discipline, all guns at the ready but pointed to the front, except for the man actually taking the shot

Before you load for the first time, look through your barrels

the place was stiff with birds. The first covey got up: my cousin swung down the line (he did not fire) and was promptly sent straight home. His disappointment was agony to see. Last day of the holidays, and so nothing to shoot at for three months and lucky if he got it then! But he was always a safe shot thereafter.

Do you ever point your gun unconsciously at someone when walking up, or simply when standing still? Your gun should either be pointed at the ground or up in the air. Is it *always*? If you do not know how to carry your gun, it will inevitably point at someone. If you do not know how to carry your gun when walking up, your left-hand neighbour will be able to 'see what size shot you are using'. In other words, your barrels will be pointing at him.

Do you *know* where people are. Certainly you do not between drives. Therefore, no shooting ever between drives, and your gun (which may

Unload when climbing a gate or hedge

or may not be put down) will be *unloaded*.

It is the low bird and the ground game that cause the danger. Be very careful, and be seen to be careful.

Driven grouse are probably the most 'dangerous' birds. They fly low and fast; there is therefore a strong tendency to swing with the bird, and you will at once break the rule if you swing too far right or left, as you will then point your gun at the next butt. You can only shoot these birds in front or behind. And certainly not even in front, when the beaters get within range.

Youngsters who are taught to shoot safely are likely to remain safe shots for life. For those who learn to shoot only when they are older, it is more difficult to learn to shoot safely. So if someone ever tells you about safety, do not take it amiss; accept it at once. He may be saving someone's life!

A bird swings right and you shoot. How close to your next-door gun?

It is quite impossible to foresee every danger. If you are ever not quite sure about a safety rule, do not be afraid to ask. People are always willing to help the seeker after knowledge, and are often flattered at being questioned. It will be clear anyway that you are a beginner, and the fact that you ask shows that you are on the right track; that you appreciate the possible danger of carelessness and inexperience, and that you are doing your best to become and be a SAFE GUN.

Etiquette

As with other similar activities, shooting has seen the evolution of certain standards of behaviour which have come, by custom, to be regarded as 'things that are done' and 'things that are not done'. This is in no sense any form of snobbery since the code of behaviour which has evolved is based squarely on safety, good manners and commonsense, and its sole purpose is to ensure the greater enjoyment of the sport by all who take part in it. Here are some of the rules of the code:

Safety: Vital always. See the preceding section.

Talking: DO NOT. I do not mean ordinary social gossip when you are not anywhere near game. But when you are waiting for, or approaching game, KEEP QUIET.

I once belonged to a syndicate one member of which was an incurable chatterer – and he had a rasping voice. I used to get all the shooting; and after a bit, it became so noticeable that I was asked about it. I never let on, but all I did was to keep away from the chatterer – well away, the other side of the wood if I could. He never got much shooting, and neither did those near him.

Do not talk when waiting for the birds or when walking up; and this includes not talking to the lovely girl friend. And it also means not yelling at your dog. The human voice frightens game, and game will not come near you, or your companions.

I sometimes had to arrive late at another shoot, where there was plenty of land. I could always find the guns because I could hear them chattering half a mile away. And if I could hear them, certainly the game could. And those guns still cannot understand why they saw plenty of birds on Friday when wandering around by themselves, yet never saw much on Saturday when they were shooting together.

Your gun should either be pointed at the ground . . .

. . . or up in the air

It is the low bird and the ground game that cause the danger. Be very careful . . .

Invitations: Accept or refuse at once. Your host wants to know because if you cannot go, he will wish to invite someone else. It makes it difficult for him, and indeed makes him appear impolite by having to give short notice, if you delay your decision.

And when you have accepted, you *must* stick to it – particularly if a better invitation comes along later for the same day.

Arrive on time: If you are asked for 9.30 am this means that you must be ready to move off then. So arrive at 9.15 so that you have time to get your boots on, gun out of its case and so on, and are all ready at 9.30 am.

Be helpful to your host: If dogs are often undisciplined and unruly, they are nothing compared to the average group of guns. One host used to say quietly once, 'Guns this way', and then walk off. For the first two drives he had the shoot of his life because none of the others were in position. They had not been polite enough to listen to their host. They were gossiping away, and just did not hear him – and so missed some very good shooting. After that, they listened, as they should have done from the start.

Listen for your host's wishes, and be the first to comply. Why should he have to struggle to get the guns moving and get the shoot started?

When you are in position, keep an eye again on your host – like a good cricket fielder watching his captain. If you are on a flank, and birds are breaking back, it simplifies your host's task if he can simply (and silently) wave you into a better position. But on no account move without his instructions.

Be helpful to your host. Volunteer for the 'walking gun', the outside berth when walking up and so on. It is at the least, good manners. And (between you and me!) you get more shooting.

Cartridges: Be sure to take enough. It is sheer bad manners to run out of cartridges; it merely implies that you thought your host could only provide a limited supply of game – certainly less than he *did* – and this is scarcely complimentary.

And fancy saving up half-days and all the rest to go shooting, and then see birds sail over your head unshot at. I remember a shoot, when I remarked before I arrived, 'I expect we'll get five shots between us all day', and the bag was 153 pheasants. I had enough cartridges and it was a splendid day . . . but supposing I had only taken enough for five shots.

Lunch: Hunger is the best sauce, good food and good fellowship all help – but do not overdo it! What goes down so easily in pleasant company at 1 pm, can sit pretty heavily when you are alone in a butt or walking up at 2.30 pm. Enjoy it, but remember that you usually eat lunch every day, whereas not all of us shoot each day. Don't spoil the rare pleasure of shooting for something you do with monotonous regularity.

Books have been written on the ideal shooting lunch. In my opinion, there is only one DON'T. Not too much starch in the shape of doorstep sandwiches, bread, buns and so on. It turns to lead after an hour in the tummy.

Hot soup in a flask can be a life saver – the colder the weather, the thicker the soup. A good slab of chocolate gives energy without bulk. Cheese, too. Put in a spare bottle or two of soda or tonic water because at the end of the day, you can have achieved a thirst you could step on! Otherwise what you like, provided it is easy to eat, and does not fall to pieces on your knees.

Guns: Be careful where you put your gun when you stop for lunch. If you lean it casually against a car or wall, it can easily be knocked over by either human stupidity or canine carelessness.

Do not put it temporarily on your car or Land Rover. You may forget, and when you drive away it will fall off; and then by some quirk of ballistics, will also be run over by the back wheels.

Look after your Gun and Equipment: Clean and oil your gun the same day as you fire it. There is a temptation on coming back tired, to 'leave it until after my bath'. And we all know that it does not then get cleaned. And what about your boots, too? Less valuable possibly than your gun, but able to be ruined slightly quicker. Neglect will ruin anything.

Numbering: At some shoots – rather the super ones – you draw a number. The number you draw is the number of your butt, or peg, for the first drive. Usually you number from the right (though not at all shoots), and your host will tell you how many guns 'you are numbering'. You usually move up two after each drive.

Thus, supposing you draw the number '1'. At the first drive, you will be the right-hand gun; then at the next drive, No 3, then No 5, then No 7, and after that No 1 if 'numbering' eight guns. You add two onto each figure after each drive – thus No 8 becomes No 2 and so on.

Remember what your number is for the first drive after lunch; this is too difficult for most people.

There are variations. Some shoots number from the left, so that No 1 is the left-hand gun. If you have seven guns, No 6 becomes No 1, and No 7 becomes No 2.

I have heard of a shoot where guns were told that odd numbers moved *up*, and even numbers moved *down* – two places, each time. This was so complicated that everybody had a card with his number for each drive. I always thought it was done to give each gun a different neighbour at each drive – a sort of 'Paul Jones', and rather friendly.

Tipping: In an age of rapid inflation, it is well nigh impossible to say 'how much'. Before the first world war, a grasping keeper knew the guns who were guests as 'Sovs' or 'Half Sovs', depending on whether they were likely to tip him a pound or ten shillings. It is a sobering thought that to be regarded as in the 'Sov' class today, you would have to tip about £10 ($25.00). We can only deduce that a keeper's income from tips has fallen in terms of real money very considerably.

Give as much as you reasonably can, and above all show your appreciation for all the work the keeper has put in, when you give it.

Beaters and Stops: Make friends with them! They are very nice people to know. They know more than you – or indeed most of the other guns – about what is going on. They also know who are the good and safe shots, and who are not. Their opinion on the day is worth having; their opinion of you and your shooting has been likened to the sort of report which would be received if the Admiralty, for example, got an opinion of a senior officer from a junior officer serving under him. A bit of an eye-opener, we all suspect.

Hares: If you shoot one, carry it if you are walking up or walking gun.

Enjoyment: Enjoy it! Be philosophical if you shoot badly (so easy to write; so very difficult to achieve). Do not excuse yourself if you have not shot well; probably no one has noticed, and certainly no one is interested. Keep your mouth shut if you are shooting well – everyone *will* have noticed! Congratulate good shooting; congratulate the poor shot on any good shot he has achieved – this is most heartening to someone who will almost certainly be depressed. And he may do the same for you one day.

DO NOT leave your gun where it can easily be knocked over by dog or human

DO NOT leave your gun where you can forget it as you drive off

Final advice

As you finish reading this book, your reaction will vary between 'What a load of rubbish' to 'Perhaps he has got something'. Let us, in charity, assume the latter!

What are you going to do about it in that case? The obvious answer is: next time you are shooting, do what is written in this book and you will become a super shot!

If it was as easy as that, most of us would be good shots. As it is, the vast majority of us are downright bad shots. For example, the number of men who kill consistently, throughout the year, more than they miss, could probably be counted on the fingers of one hand. (This, I admit, is not the right way to judge the skill of a shot, but at least it is an indication of the very bad standard of shooting.)

For some reason, very few people practise shooting. At no other sport or skill, do you get such a state of affairs. The golfer who slogs away, the pianist who practises for hours every day – they all do it. Yet if we see a good shot out, all we say is 'So he ought to be; look at the practice he gets'. We are, I suppose, jealous. But if we do not take steps to improve our shooting, we may well ask what we are shooting for.

Basically, we are too lazy. If this is true of you, you will try and kid yourself that reading this book is enough. It is quite easy to read a book – we have all practised reading enough! 'He will improve my shooting' you may say. You will make the fundamental mistake of not realising that it is *your* finger on the trigger, *your* arms and hands mounting the gun, and *your* body moving the gun to the bird.

In short, you cannot get away with this lazy way out. Sooner or later you have got to try and make your body comply with the wishes of your brain, which we are charitably assuming has been favourably influenced by reading this book. You have got to get down physically to putting into practice what you have read, and agreed with. You must try it out, and above all practise what your brain – and only your brain – has absorbed.

There are three reasons for this. First, you may honestly believe you are doing something I have told you, yet you are *not*. Another reason is that you accept my advice with reservations; and the last reason is that you do not absorb (or you misunderstand) what you are being told.

To give an example of the last point: the non-absorption of information. I was coaching a young man, and he was shooting at some approaching clays. I was trying to get him to *push* his gun at them; he was *lifting* his gun, and thus could not and did not, keep with them as he mounted. Before every shot, I told him to push the gun at them. After twenty counted shots, I got exasperated, and held the gun near the breech when he was about to mount the gun. When the clay came over, I pushed the gun towards the clay to give him the feeling I was trying to instil. He pulled the trigger and broke the clay. He then turned to me and said, 'Oh, I see. Push the gun towards the bird. Why didn't you say so!' I wonder what he was thinking about before.

You will accept what I say with reservations. We all do it. A quick example – a shooting coach has told you that you mount your gun correctly to your cheek and shoulder. What he meant was that the gun was correctly mounted when it got there. He did *not* mean that you mounted correctly with the bird; you thought he did mean just that. So you skip the bit about gun mounting; and you get no better at shooting.

The last point: that you are not doing what you think you are. I have had much experience of this, but I will give only two examples.

'Mount the gun with the bird,' I say. After most people have fired at, say a 'driven partridge' medium height, coming towards, I ask them whether they thought they were with it all the time they mounted. In all sincerity, they say 'Yes'. What they *did* do was to snatch the butt into the shoulder and cheek, down went the barrels, and if they had fired half way through mounting they would have hit the ground in front of them. I point out that the bird was never there.

I am not believed.

So I hold (from behind) the whip aerial of my 'walkie-talkie' under the gun barrels, so that if the barrels go down instead of forward and up with the bird, they will hit the aerial. When the barrels *do* hit the aerial, I am accused of flipping the aerial up to make them raise the barrels. None so blind as those who won't see!

Are *you* blind – deliberately?

Studying the pictures in this book of the correct and incorrect ways of standing etc, very few of us will visualise ourselves in any of the incorrect positions. We always associate with the hero – a Walter Mitty complex.

The really important point is not whether you have ever been in one of the incorrect positions; it is how many of the incorrect positions you always adopt.

Be humble. Try to see yourself as others see you . . . and become a good shot!

Vital allies for a good day's sport – dogs and pickers-up, who know more than most what is going on, not to mention who can shoot well

At the end of the day: a superb bag

Glossary of Shooting Terms

Automatics The same as a 'pump' gun (qv), except that the re-cocking and ejection cycle is performed automatically by recoil or gas pressure.

Box Lock A simple robust action, easily adjusted or repaired. Sometimes known as the Anson & Deeley system. Introduced in 1875. See under *Locks*.

British Proof It is illegal to sell any gun that has not been 'proofed'. Every British gun has to go to a Proof House, where an abnormally heavy charge is fired from each barrel. If this test is passed, the barrel is stamped accordingly. A barrel can subsequently become 'out of proof' through wear.

Cast-Off The wooden stock of an English gun is often bent out sideways to the right in the case of a right-handed gun to enable the butt to fit firmly into the shoulder, and at the same time for the barrels to point where the eye is looking.

Cast-On Is where the stock is bent to the left, for a left-handed gun, and for the same reason.

Choke A constriction at the end of the barrel, which in the case of 'full choke' amounts to 40/1,000 of an inch. The other extreme is True Cylinder, a term which is self-explanatory. Improved Cylinder has a small degree of constriction. The object is to concentrate the shot into a smaller area and thus increase the effective range; the greater the choke, the greater reduction in the spread of the shot.

Down the Line A specific clay pigeon sport. Clays are thrown at varying angles away from the gun, who is sixteen yards (or more) from the trap. The gun can be mounted in the shoulder and the clay is released when called for by the shooter.

Driven Game The beaters drive the game towards the guns who are thus offered shots at birds which may have got up a long way back, and so be flying fast and high. This type of shooting generally offers more sporting and difficult shots.

Locks The lock of a gun is responsible for causing the striker to go forward and fire the cartridge when the trigger is pulled. It also ensures that the striker is pulled back and cocked when the gun is opened, and retained in this position until the trigger is again pulled.

Mark! A warning shout that game is approaching.

Over and Under Double-barrel guns with their barrels placed one on top of the other. Used most often in clay pigeon shooting, for which sport they can be more easily 'aimed'. A tendency to be rather heavy, and wide opening to allow the lower barrel to be loaded, means that not many are used for game shooting.

Pattern Guns are usually tested for pattern by firing them at a whitewashed iron plate at forty yards distance. The shot marks should be evenly distributed; the concentration of the pattern is determined by the percentage of the pellets in a 30in diameter circle.

'Pump' Gun A single-barrel repeating gun. The gun is re-cocked and the 'empty' ejected by pulling back the sliding fore-end. Usually can be loaded with five rounds, but this takes a long time. Rather clumsy to handle.

Right and Left When a bird is shot with the right barrel, followed immediately by a kill with the left barrel, without re-loading.

Side Lock Probably the best (and most expensive) form of lock, and the oldest. Capable of very fine adjustment, and is utterly reliable and safe. A refined and thoroughbred version of the box lock.

Skeet Shooting A type of sporting clay pigeon shooting. There are two traps opposite each other, with the trapper suitably protected. One trap is about 20ft high and the other 10ft high; one clay is thrown towards the other trap, when called for, and the second clay released in the opposite direction on the report of the gun.

Gun positions are in a semi-circle with the first position near the higher trap. This position thus gets a going-away shot, followed immediately by a lower incomer. The halfway position gives a left to right crosser, followed by a right to left crosser. Quick shooting at comparatively short ranges is required.

Springing Teal A type of clay pigeon shot in which the clay is thrown upwards at an angle of 70°. Released and shot at in the same way as Down the Line.

Stop When game is driven towards the guns, pheasants in particular will take every opportunity of getting away by running down a ditch or hedgerow (instead of flying). A man thus placed strategically and tapping with a stick will prevent such escapes.

Walking Gun Where beaters are driving game towards the guns, it is sometimes necessary to have a gun walking with the beaters, to shoot birds breaking back, or flying out to one side.

Walking Up The guns and beaters walk in line, the guns shooting at birds thus disturbed. Mostly going-away shots.

Appendices

I – How to see the Shot!

That anybody can actually see shot fired from a shotgun, travelling through the air, strikes the majority of us as being simply incredible. And yet it can be done and, in fact, is being done pretty well every day throughout the year.

How else could the shotgun coach advise his pupil what he is doing wrong, unless he can see the shot in the air? 'Oh, well' you say. 'You are talking about an expert, who has done this all his life. They must have eyes like hawks'.

This is not true. Anyone, young or old, with reasonable eyesight can learn to see the shot quite easily. There is, of course, one important proviso, which I will come to in a minute. But subject to this proviso, the ability to see this phenomenon can be acquired readily, and it can be incredibly useful.

Usually anybody can be taught – the man, who as you get older, carries your gun and cartridges: your friend, or your loader (with one qualification), if you are fortunate enough to shoot somewhere with sufficient birds to require two guns. It is an enormous help – almost unfair; and yet no one ever thinks of having his loader/companion or whatever, taught how to see the shot.

I must at this stage get the qualifications and proviso that I have mentioned, out of the way. The qualification is that the loader is there to load: he cannot always watch your shot and load. Bear this in mind in a hot corner when he says he 'didn't see', in answer to your frantic shout for help.

The proviso is that you cannot see your own shot. The reason is that as the shot emerges, there is an appreciable flash, and this prevents your sighting the shot. There *is* a flash – not noticeable by day, but only too apparent at night.

In spite of this, I have, in fact seen my own shot on several occasions. The reason probably is that the gun butt was so far away from my cheek (and the gun as a result pointing nowhere near the target), that I could see round the flash.

Now how to see the shot. The first absolute essential is not to flinch at the bang. Of course you don't: you have been out shooting for years, and the thought is laughable. But you do, ever so slightly, and this is enough. Watch someone shooting, and he nearly always blinks slightly at the bang and quite unknowingly his eyes are probably closing – or closed! – as the shot leaves the barrel. Cultivate the mentality of the shooting instructor who has reached the stage where each discharge barely registers.

Stand fairly close behind the 'gun', and try to get into a position so that his mounted weapon is roughly in line with your eye. Naturally your eye will have to be above the line of the gun, and clear of the obstructing flash. Look firmly at the target – we will assume it is a clay, as clay pigeon shooting is as good a place as any to learn – and, if you do not blink, you will see the shot as a dark blur, going incredibly quickly. If it hits the clay you will probably not see the shot in the air, but it then does not matter! With practice, the shot can be seen quite clearly every time and, as you acquire the knack, from practically any position behind the gun.

On crossing shots, the dark blur of the pattern will appear to curve away behind the target. This is an optical illusion, and will clearly be remembered by anyone who fired anti-aircraft tracer in the last war.

If you miss the blur, you can very often tell where the shot missed, by the 'feel' of the gun as the shooter mounts it. You can often see that he is starting, say, left of the target, keeps there as he mounts, and finally misses there. Or, on another occasion, you can feel him mount badly, and then try and catch up with a frantic flick ahead, and duly miss there. It is so easy to shoot well when you are standing behind the chap who is actually shooting.

The spectator sees more of the game. This can, indeed, be most true of the sport about which we are talking. But nearly everyone is convinced that he cannot see the shot, or believes that only a chosen few can do it, and so he does not even try.

It is almost 'unfairly' helpful to you as a gun, if you can get reliable advice as to where your shot is going. Your spectator companion can so easily learn. In fact, he is more than half way there if he reads this.

II – Pattern and Killing Power

Table 1

Minimum Patterns (including allowance for stringing)

Game	Minimum Pattern in a 30in circle
Snipe	270
Woodcock	150
Squirrel	180
Partridge	130
Grouse	130
Pheasant	120
Pigeon	130
Rabbit	120
Teal	110
Hare	100
Duck	80
Goose	70

Table 2

Percentage Patterns for all Borings at all Ranges

Boring of gun	Range in yards						
	30	35	40	45	50	55	60
True Cyl.	60	49	40	33	27	22	18
Imp. Cyl.	72	60	50	41	33	27	22
$\frac{1}{4}$-Choke	77	65	55	46	38	30	25
$\frac{1}{2}$-Choke	83	71	60	50	41	33	27
$\frac{3}{4}$-Choke	91	77	65	55	46	37	30
Full Choke	100	84	70	59	49	40	32

Table 3

Striking Energy in ft-lb for Individual Pellets fired at Observed Velocity of 1,070ft per sec

Size of shot	Range in yards 30	35	40	45	50	55	60
3	4.48	3.92	3.43	2.99	2.59	2.23	1.94
4	3.54	3.08	2.66	2.30	1.97	1.68	1.42
5	2.60	2.23	1.90	1.61	1.36	1.14	0.93
6	2.03	1.71	1.44	1.20	1.01	0.82	0.67
7	1.52	1.27	1.06	0.86	0.70	0.57	0.45

Table 4

Diameter of Spread
(being the diameter in inches covered by the bulk of the charge of a gun at various ranges for all calibres*)

Boring of gun	Range in yards 10	15	20	25	30	35	40
True Cyl.	20	26	32	38	44	51	58
Imp. Cyl.	15	20	26	32	38	44	51
¼-Choke	13	18	23	29	35	41	48
½-Choke	12	16	21	26	32	38	45
¾-Choke	10	14	18	23	29	35	42
Full Choke	9	12	16	21	27	33	40

* SPECIAL NOTE: Because of the persistent fallacy that small-bore guns throw a smaller pattern circle than those of larger bore, it is necessary to emphasise that this is not the case. All bores throw approximately the same diameter circle, and the above table is therefore true for all calibres as stated.

III – Suggested Rules for a Clay Pigeon Club

1 The title of the club shall be the '................Clay Pigeon Club'.
2 The headquarters of the club shall be at ....
3 The object and aim of the club shall be to improve the standard of game shooting among members.
4 The management of the club shall be vested in a chairman and in a committee of five, three of whom shall form a quorum, who shall be elected from the members of the club at each annual general meeting. Retiring members shall be eligible for re-election.
5 A president and vice-president shall be elected from the members of the club at each annual general meeting, and the retiring president and vice-president shall be eligible for re-election.
6 The committee shall have the power to add to the number of vice-presidents for the current year.
7 An honorary treasurer and honorary secretary shall be elected from the members at each annual general meeting, and the retiring honorary treasurer and honorary secretary shall be eligible for re-election.
8 The committee have power to fill any vacancies on the committee during the current year, and also have power to form sub-committees as may be required for special purposes.
9 The president and vice-president shall be ex-officio members of the committee, but the vice-president shall not have voting powers. The honorary treasurer and honorary secretary shall be ex-officio members of all committees with full voting powers.
10 All monies received on behalf of the club shall forthwith be paid into the account of the club at the .... Bank. The honorary treasurer shall have power to draw on such account, and no cheque shall be drawn by him unless countersigned by another official and previously sanctioned by resolution of the committee. No prizes or other articles shall be purchased, or debts or liabilities incurred on behalf of the club by any person, without the previous sanction of a resolution of the committee or at the general meeting of the club.
11 The accounts of the club shall be audited every year by auditors to be appointed at a general meeting of the club. A copy of the accounts so audited shall be sent to every member of the club at least seven days before the annual general meeting of the club.
12 The annual subscription of the club shall be two guineas per annum, with an entrance fee of two guineas for the first year. The financial year of the club shall be from 1 April until 31 March the following year.
13 The annual general meeting of the club shall be held on or after the last week in March each year, and fourteen days' notice shall be given to all

members. Resolutions to be proposed at the meeting shall be given in writing to the honorary secretary seven clear days before the date of the meeting.

14 On a petition signed by at least one-third of the members of the club being presented in writing to the honorary secretary, a special general meeting shall be called within fourteen days from the date of presentation of the petition to consider the matter contained therein.

15 The committee shall have power to form such bye-laws as they consider will be conductive to the good of the club, and to the encouragement of this sport.

16 A candidate for election shall be proposed and seconded by members of the club, who shall submit his name and address to the committee. The committee shall vote thereon at the first committee meeting subsequent to the one at which his application for membership was submitted, unless the committee unanimously resolve to vote thereon at the committee meeting at which such application was received by them.

17 Any member whose subscription is unpaid from 1 May shall not be allowed any of the privileges of membership. The committee may strike out names of members whose subscriptions are more than two months in arrears.

18 Members shall, subject to the consent of all members present, have the right of introducing visitors to practice, provided any members introducing a visitor shall be liable for all debts incurred by him to the club. No visitors shall be invited to practise or shoot more than three times in the same season. No member may introduce more than two visitors at the same time.

19 The committee shall be empowered to request the resignation of a member if it be proved to their satisfaction that his conduct merits it; and in the event of his failing to resign, the committee may suspend such member without further notice. The resolution calling on a member to be suspended should be carried by the votes of the majority of the members present and voting, notwithstanding anything herein contained to the contrary as regards a quorum or otherwise. Such a suspension may only be reviewed at a general meeting.

20 Members must use such targets as may be decided upon by the club.

21 A range officer approved by the committee must be appointed for each club shoot.

22 It is a condition of membership that the club will not be held responsible (except as covered by insurance), for any accident and/or injury occurring to or caused by either members or visitors.

23 The committee is empowered to make or alter any rule which may be found necessary to conform with the Licensing (Consolidation) Act 1910, and such rule shall forthwith become a rule of the club as if it had been passed at a general meeting.

24 These rules shall be open to revision during the first year of the club by the committee, but after that no alteration shall be made except by resolution at the annual general meeting.

25 Temporary members may be elected for a period of one month. They must be proposed and seconded by a member and elected by the committee. The fee for such membership shall be 52½p.

26 In the event of the club being disbanded all the assets of the club shall be liquidated and equally divided among the full members on the books of the club at that date.

Acknowledgements

Pictures on pp 38–9 by John & James Marchington, Great Bookham, Surrey, and Roy Shaw, Cottingham, E Yorks; pp 80, 81, 84–7 by courtesy of James Purdey & Sons Ltd; pp 90–1, 94–5, 110–11 by Roy Shaw; other pictures copyright of the author.

Index

David & Charles have a book on it

A Guide to Rough Shooting, by Arthur Cadman. An authority on British deer and wildfowl distils years of experience of shooting over every kind of rough ground. A book of particular value to the young shot, to whom is devoted a special chapter. Well laced with amusing and often informative anecdotes. Illustrated.

Training Pointers and Setters by J. B. Maurice. That the ancient art of training gundogs can be learned from a book is ably demonstrated by Dr Maurice, who has himself had considerable successes with pointers and setters. He covers breeding, choosing a puppy, domestication and health hazards, and the basics of educating a gundog for a typical shooting day. Illustrated.

Crossbows by Frank Bilson. For many people the urge to shoot is stifled by the rising cost of going out with the guns. Competitive target shooting with one of man's earliest weapons – the crossbow – is proving an excellent alternative. In the first book to be written on crossbows since the beginning of the century, Frank Bilson provides a fascinatingly detailed introduction to a sport which is fast gaining new enthusiasts throughout the world. Illustrated.

Still-Water Angling by Richard Walker. Hailed as revolutionary when it first appeared in 1953, this book is still a firmly-established classic of angling literature. This new edition incorporates much additional information gleaned by the author and his friends since the book was first published. Illustrated.

By River, Stream and Loch: Thirty Years with a Trout Rod by A. R. B. Haldane. With its delightful wood-cuts by Helen Monro Turner, this is a book written entirely for pleasure, and the quality of the writing makes angling exciting and intelligible to non-anglers as well. Illustrated.

UNIFORM WITH THIS VOLUME: Archery for All by Daniel Roberts. Following the style and presentation of *The Art of Good Shooting*, with its concise text supplemented by profuse illustrations, this is the ideal introduction to the sport of archery. Ideal for all ages, it does not forget the disabled. Illustrated.

Coarse Fishing for New Anglers by W. M. Hill. A practical introduction to the sport of coarse fishing for keen beginners of all ages, this book has been designed to take the reader easily and interestingly through the progressive stages if his angling apprenticeship – an ideal guide to one of the most popular of all outdoor sports, and an introduction to the hobby of a lifetime. Illustrated.

THE FIELD Bedside Book 4, edited by Wilson Stephens. Another selection of the most popular articles from two years' issues of *The Field* magazine, with styles ranging from the straightforward and gently reflective to tongue in cheek and downright amusing. The perfect gift and an ideal read for all lovers of the countryside and its ways.